Song of Songs

Books in the Bible Study Commentary Series

*Not yet published as of this printing

BIBLE STUDY COMMENTARY

Song of Songs

EDWARD M. CURTIS

Lamplighter
Books Grand Rapids,
Michigan
Zondervan Publishing House

Song of Songs: Bible Study Commentary

Lamplighter Books are published by the Zondervan Publishing House, 1415 Lake Drive, S.E., Grand Rapids, Michigan 49506

Library of Congress Cataloging in Publication Data

Curtis, Edward M.
    Song of songs.

    (Bible study commentary)
    Bibliography: p.
    1. Bible. O.T. Song of Solomon—Commentaries.
I. Title. II. Series: Bible study commentary series.
BS1485.3.C87   1988   223'.907   87-27942
ISBN 0-310-36871-5

Edited by Nia Jones, John D. Sloan

Printed in the United States of America

88 89 90 91 92 / EP / 10 9 8 7 6 5 4 3 2 1

*In praise and gratitude
to my Beloved, Joy.*

Acknowledgments

Special appreciation is due to Biola University and Talbot School of Theology for granting me a one semester sabbatical leave to work on this project.

Contents

Abbreviations

AB	Anchor Bible
ASV	American Standard Version
JB	Jerusalem Bible
NASB	New American Standard Bible
NIV	New International Version
RSV	Revised Standard Version
TOTC	Tyndale Old Testament Commentary

Part 1

Introductory Matters

Chapter 1

Introduction

There is no book of the Bible (including the Book of Revelation) that has been discussed as extensively[1] and about which there continues to be so much disagreement as the Song of Solomon (or Song of Songs, as it is known in the Hebrew Bible), and there are a variety of reasons for this. Some of the disagreement results from its unusual vocabulary. Over one third of the words either occur only here or occur so infrequently in the Hebrew Bible that their exact meaning cannot be determined. Many of these words are names of plants, perfumes, etc. Although uncertainty about the exact meaning of the words does not keep us from understanding the passage in which they occur, the large number of obscure words has contributed to many uncertainties in understanding various details of this biblical book.

Likewise, its subject matter has resulted in many different opinions about how Song of Songs is to be understood. It is clear that the book describes the love relationship between a man and a woman, and the description includes the physical and sexual part of the relationship. Some commentators have struggled with this material, which, understood at face value, seemed unworthy of inclusion in Holy Scripture. Many have advocated an interpretation that elevated its meaning above the apparent and

---

[1]Marvin Pope's *Anchor Bible Commentary* on Song of Songs which was published in 1977 includes a fifty-five page bibliography that includes some thirteen hundred items. This bibliography is by no means complete and would be extended considerably by the publications from the past ten years.

literal meaning of the figures and have suggested that the book was meant primarily to describe the relationship between the Lord and His people (either Israel, the church, or the individual believer). Some of these interpreters have argued that the events described actually took place historically (the typological interpretation), while others have suggested that the story was simply created to teach a significant spiritual truth (the allegorical interpretation). Both these approaches are agreed that the plain sense of the text is not the primary meaning of the text, and their basic reasoning seems to be the supposition that human love, including its physical and sensual aspects, is not a topic worthy of inclusion in divinely inspired Scripture.

Many others have concluded that the Song does describe the love between a man and a woman; however, this conclusion has not produced agreement about the purpose of the book. Although the book consists of a number of different poems, these are not connected by a narrative framework, which clearly tells the story of the lovers. Therefore, some have suggested that there is no story and that the book is simply a collection of separate poems written by various authors at different times. One possible purpose of this anthology is to celebrate the beauty and virtue of human love; another possibility is that these poems were used in connection with wedding ceremonies in ancient Israel.

However, there are expressions and themes that recur throughout the book and suggest its unity and the probability of a connected story. At the same time, it is not clear exactly what that story is. The text does not clearly identify the speaker in every dialogue in the book (The fact that Hebrew uses different forms for referring to men and women helps in determining the speaker.) and there is often debate over who is speaking in specific verses. Nevertheless, it is clear that certain assumptions must be made to construct a unified story from the poetry, and commentators have suggested several different stories that they feel are consistent with the contents of poetry in the Song.

While Solomon's exact relationship to the book is a matter of considerable discussion, he is mentioned several times in the book, and it seems likely that the story involves his relationship with a woman. Many have understood the Song in this way, but the fact that Solomon does not seem like an appropriate model for the ideal relationship between a man and a woman poses a problem for this view. Some have suggested that the book describes Solomon's relationship with his first wife or with a wife whom he truly loved as opposed to the foreign wives whom he married for political expediency. Others have suggested that Solomon is not the hero of the book and that there are three major characters rather than two. According to this view, a young girl who was in love with a shepherd from the area where she lived was taken to Jerusalem by Solomon to become a part of his harem. Despite the splendor of the court and the benefit that she would realize by being Solomon's wife, the girl rejected Solomon's advances and was finally allowed to return to her true love.

Some have proposed the theory that this material had its ultimate origins in the fertility cults, which flourished in the ancient world and existed in Israel despite the condemnation of such practices in the Law and the Prophets. This theory does little to further the understanding of the present biblical book but has become more popular as a result of several recent commentaries espousing it.

Some of these theories can be rejected either on textual or theological grounds; others can be dismissed as unlikely. Several remain as possibilities, however, and perhaps to a greater degree than with any other book of the Bible it is impossible to present a particular view of the book as THE correct interpretation. As Jack Deere has noted in his recent study of Song of Songs, "This particular reading of the Song is offered as one among several that are plausible and defensible from the text itself without unduly 'straining' the meaning of the text or 'reading into' the text what is not there."[2]

The great variety of opinion about the Song and the differences of opinion about almost every aspect of it make it essential to devote more discussion to introductory matters than would normally be the case in a commentary of this type. Conclusions about the kind of literature, the nature of the

---

[2] Jack S. Deere, "The Meaning of the Song of Songs: An Historical and Exegetical Inquiry" (unpublished Th.D. dissertation, Dallas Theological Seminary, 1984), p. 2.

language and metaphors, the major point taught by the book, the story recounted in the book, etc., must, of course, result from a careful study of the text itself. In the case of the Song of Solomon, these decisions cannot be made entirely on that basis, since even the most careful study will leave us with several possibilities, which *may* be, rather than with one conclusion, which *must* be. At the same time, it is clear that decisions about these matters will be applied to the text of the book and will determine the interpretation of various details throughout the book. Again, this makes it imperative to identify for the reader the issues that are involved in these decisions and to encourage the careful consideration of these preliminary questions throughout the study of this book.

A. The Date of the Song

The references to Solomon in 1:1, 5; 3:7, 9, 11 and 8:11, 12 appear to provide a clear objective basis for dating this book somewhere near the middle of the tenth century B.C., and this is the view that prevailed among both Christian and Jewish commentators prior to the nineteenth century and the beginning of critical biblical scholarship. Today many scholars question the traditional date largely on the basis of linguistic evidence that suggests a later date for the book. There are certain grammatical features that are more common in a later period than the time of Solomon (though some of these may reflect the influence of the dialect of Hebrew spoken in the North) and there are certain words that may have been borrowed into Hebrew from Persian or Greek. At the same time, there are some grammatical features that seem to require an early date, so the linguistic evidence is at best ambiguous.[3] There is little objective evidence beyond the references to Solomon that would make it possible to determine a date, and there is nothing except the linguistic evidence that poses a significant problem for a mid-tenth century B.C. date.

Those who view the book as an anthology determine the

---

[3] Pope's summary of opinions about the date of the book (pp. 22–33) makes it clear that a number of scholars who dismiss the significance of the references to Solomon still date the book in the Solomonic era. It is evident that they do not see the linguistic evidence as precluding such a date.

date of each separate poem on the basis of the evidence in that poem and generally see the book as having been put together from poetry of different periods, ranging from well before the time of Solomon to the post-Exilic period. Many would date the final editing of the book in the second or third century B.C.; however, fragments of the book among the Dead Sea Scrolls set a limit for how late this compilation could have occurred.

Those who argue for the unity of the book find strong evidence for a date in the references to Solomon. The references in 1:5 and perhaps those in 8:11–12 do not necessarily connect the events described with the historical figure Solomon, but those in 3:7, 9, 11 do appear to make that connection. The mention of Solomon in 1:1 also connects Solomon in some way with the events described, even if it does not identify him as the author of the poetry.

Those who feel that the linguistic evidence, despite its ambiguity, requires a later date for the book generally suggest that the book is similar to a historical novel because a later author used Solomon as the major character and the Solomonic age as the "ideal" setting for his work. The book may reflect a story that had been preserved about Solomon, perhaps the traditional ideal or ultimate lover, or it may simply describe what "might have been." The public perception about Solomon may have made him a suitable character for effectively making the point that the author wanted to make.

If, as seems probable, the book is a unity, the references to Solomon clearly establish the setting for the book as the mid-tenth century B.C., and apart from the theory that the book is a later literary composition that projects itself back to the time of Solomon, it seems likely that the book was actually composed during the time of Solomon or soon thereafter. It is possible that the linguistic features taken by many to be characteristic of the Hebrew during the late post-Exilic period are characteristic of a northern Hebrew dialect;[4] it is also possible that some modern-

---

[4] All do not agree that these linguistic features necessarily point to a late date. Gleason Archer (*A Survey of Old Testament Introduction*, [Chicago: Moody Press, 1964], pp. 473–74) argues that these features can be explained apart from the conclusion that they are indicative of later Hebrew.

izing of the language in the book took place at a later time.[5] Thus, while this view is not free from all problems, it seems probable that Song of Songs was written during the middle part of the tenth century B.C.

B. The Authorship of the Song

The question of the authorship of Song of Songs is closely connected with the decisions reached about the date of the book, the unity of the book, and the story told in the book. Those who view the book as an anthology of poems generally conclude that the separate poems were written by a number of different people over a long period of time. Those who conclude that the book consists of a unified story will be greatly influenced by their conclusion about the date of the book and their understanding of the story.

The book begins with a statement that many believe identifies Solomon as the author of the book ("Solomon's Song of Songs," NIV), and the Hebrew preposition used here is a common way of indicating authorship. The preposition, though, can mean a number of things, and here it could just as easily mean "the Song of Songs about Solomon" or "for Solomon" or "commissioned by Solomon." Thus a decision about authorship will have to be made on some basis other than this statement. Obviously, those who date the book later than the tenth century B.C. will reject the possibility of Solomonic authorship. If, as we have suggested, the book was written in the tenth century B.C., the decision will depend to some degree on how the story of the book is understood. Those who see Solomon as the villain (the shepherd hypothesis) rather than the hero will conclude that Solomon is not likely the author of the book; many who see the story as involving two major characters (Solomon and the girl) will conclude that Solomon is probably the author of the work.

Solomonic authorship cannot be proved, but it is consistent

---

[5]Some support for this idea *may* be found in the Jewish tradition that "Hezekiah and his company . . . wrote Song of Songs" (*Mishnah, Baba Bathra* 15a). It has been suggested by G. L. Carr (*The Song of Songs*, Tyndale Old Testament Commentaries, [Downers Grove, Illinois: Inter-Varsity Press, 1984], p. 18, n. 1) that this describes a process similar to that indicated in Proverbs 25:1, where proverbial material attributed to Solomon was copied (perhaps collected/edited?) by Hezekiah's scribes.

with what is known about his literary pursuits[6] and interest in the natural realm.[7] Perhaps the major objection to Solomonic authorship, other than the linguistic features that suggest a later date as discussed above, is the fact that Solomon's own example as a husband (According to 1 Kings 11:3, he had seven hundred wives and three hundred concubines.) seems to preclude the possibility that he could be a role model for the ideal love relationship between a man and a woman. It has been suggested that the relationship described here involved Solomon's "true love" in contrast to the wives he married for political expediency or that this was his first wife who died. It is also possible that this book describes an ideal relationship that Solomon never experienced. Certainly, Solomon failed to live on the basis of the proverbial material that he originated and collected, and his awareness of the way God intended things to work between a man and a woman was never applied either. Thus, Solomonic authorship of this book seems as plausible as any other possibility, and it may well be that the Spirit-illuminated wisdom of Solomon allowed him to describe an ideal relationship that he never experienced because of his refusal to apply the truth that he knew.

For Further Study

1. Read about Solomon's wisdom in 1 Kings 3:5–28 and 4:29–34.

2. Read about Solomon's marriages in 1 Kings 11:1–13.

---

[6] 1 Kings 4:32 says that Solomon "spoke" 3,000 proverbs and 1,005 songs.

[7] It must be pointed out, however, that the love poetry of the ancient Near East (and from elsewhere as well) contains many figures taken from the realm of nature. These figures and themes are so characteristic of this kind of literature that they are of limited value in determining the authorship of the Song.

Chapter 2

The Interpretation of the Song

An almost infinite variety of interpretations have been proposed for Song of Songs, and only a brief summary of the major approaches can be given here.[1]

A. Allegory

Allegory is a kind of literature in which incidents and characters in one realm actually represent those in a different realm. Sometimes, political and historical figures are described through stories that on the surface have little to do with the actual events but that clearly depict the historical and political reality. An example of this is found in Judges 9, where Jotham describes Abimelech's attempt to become king of Israel through a story about the trees of the forest. Often, allegory is used to emphasize a moral or spiritual point, and perhaps the best known example is John Bunyan's *Pilgrim's Progress* in which the spiritual conflicts and ultimate victory of the faithful believer are described through the story of Christian's journey from the City of Destruction to the Celestial City.

In view of the nature and often the purpose of allegory it seems essential that the connection between the figure and the deeper reality be only thinly veiled for the underlying point to

---

[1] For more comprehensive summaries of the history of interpretation of Song of Solomon see Christian D. Ginsburg, *The Song of Songs and Coheleth*, with a Prolegomenon by Sheldon Blank (New York: KTAV Publishing House, 1970), pp. xxxv-xliv and 20–124; Pope, AB, pp. 89–229; H. H. Rowley, "The Interpretation of the Song of Songs," in *The Servant of the Lord and Other Essays on the Old Testament* (Oxford: Blackwell, 1965), pp. 189–235.

be clear to the reader. Certainly, place names like Doubting Castle and Vanity Fair constitute obvious clues to the allegorical nature of Bunyan's story. Biblical allegories, like Judges 9 or Isaiah 5:1–7 or Psalm 80:8–17 or Ezekiel 16, contain obvious indications either in the text or the context to make it clear that they are allegories. In contrast to this, there are no clear indications that Song of Songs was intended as an allegory. Apart from the fact that the figure of the marriage relationship is a common biblical figure for describing the relationship between God and His people, there is little to suggest that the Song was written as an allegory. The places mentioned are real places, such as Jerusalem, Tirzah, Mt. Hermon, En-Gedi; Solomon is a well-known historical figure. The names mentioned do not appear to have meanings that would suggest some hidden significance beyond the apparent reference to the place or person. Therefore, the Song is entirely lacking the kind of obvious clues normally found in the kind of literature known as allegory.

Even when a piece of literature was not intended as an allegory, it is possible for an interpreter to understand it in that way, and the allegorical interpretation of Song of Solomon has played a prominent role in the history of the exegesis of the book.

Allegorical interpretation can be done in a number of ways and for a number of reasons. Paul, for instance, interprets the story of Sarah and Hagar as an allegory in Galatians 4:21–31 and simply draws a spiritual point from the historical incident. Allegorical interpretation was also used by various Greek philosophers as they sought to make older popular Greek writings more acceptable to educated Greeks, who would find the literal sense of those texts offensive. According to Carr, "These philosophers denied the historical reality and obvious teachings of the older writers. . . . The stories of the gods were not to be taken literally, they argued, but were only vehicles to convey the real hidden or secret meanings which the commentators knew."[2] This method of interpretation was later used by

---

[2] Carr, TOTC, p. 22.

certain biblical interpreters and became popular among both Christian and Jewish interpreters.

Since interpreters did not confine the use of this method to problematic passages, it cannot be supposed that it was adopted by Christian and Jewish interpreters for the same reasons that it seems to have been developed by some of the Greeks. At the same time, it seems certain that a major appeal to an allegorizing interpretation of Song of Songs had to do with the fact that this method provided a way of removing the sensual and erotic figures in the book by changing them into profound spiritual and theological truths. The possibility that the love between a man and a woman, including the physical and sexual expression of that love, could in and of itself be an appropriate and worthy topic for inclusion in Scripture was almost universally rejected by both Jewish and Christian interpreters prior to the Reformation. Christian interpreters, unlike their Jewish counterparts, were dominated by a perspective that encouraged celibacy and monasticism as the ultimate expression of spirituality; therefore, this ensured the vigorous rejection of any suggestion that a book of the Bible could celebrate and encourage the pleasures of human love between a man and a woman.[3]

The allegorical interpretation of the Song views it as describing the relationship between God (the bridegroom) and His people (Israel, the church or the individual believer). Sometimes this is understood in terms of the general development of the relationship; other times it is understood in terms of the developing history of Israel/the church. The allegorical method finds a spiritual meaning in the figures and incidents throughout the book, and the apparent reference to the human relationship between a man and a woman is rejected as a carnal understanding. Illustrative of this approach to the Song are the following examples taken from Rowley.[4] Origen understood the

---

[3] As both Rowley ("Interpretation," pp. 206–8) and Pope (AB, pp. 112–32) point out, those who suggested a literal interpretation of the Song were not viewed kindly by many in the church, and several were condemned for their views. The presupposition that the praise of human love could not be a proper topic for inspired Scripture is further seen in the fact that several of the interpreters who concluded that the book should be interpreted literally also concluded that the book, therefore, should not be included in Holy Scripture.

[4] Rowley, "Interpretation," pp. 192–200.

girl's statement in 1:5 "Dark am I but lovely" to mean dark with sin but lovely through conversion. Philo Carpasius took these words of 7:2 "Your navel is a rounded goblet that never lacks blended wine" to refer to the sanctuary of the church, while Hengstenberg understood the same words as referring to the cup from which the church revives the thirsty with its refreshing draught.

The subjective nature of this method contributes to an almost infinite variety of interpretations suggested by its advocates, and this lack of objective control constitutes a major objection to the method. It often appears that the only limits to interpretation based on this method are those imposed by the ingenuity and creativity of the interpreter, and the inability of interpreters using this approach to agree as to what the Song means seriously undermines its credibility. Most advocates of this approach begin with the presupposition that the relationship between a man and a woman could not be the focus of the book and thus conclude that it must have been intended as allegory, but this does not seem to be a necessary presupposition.

It must be pointed out, however, that this method of interpreting the book has been the dominant one throughout most of the history of the church (and perhaps prior to that as well). Many of the great men of biblical scholarship and piety have interpreted the book allegorically, and this interpretive method has resulted in the edification of many believers through the centuries. It appears though that an important distinction must be made between what is devotionally helpful and what is exegetically correct. Many of the points affirmed by interpreters of the Song seem to be biblically correct principles that can be supported from other passages of Scripture; it seems very doubtful, that these points can be exegetically derived from the text of the Song of Solomon. The dangers inherent in the allegorical method of interpretation appear to constitute a legitimate basis for rejecting it as the proper way of interpreting the Song.

B. Typology

The typological interpretation of Song of Songs is quite similar to the allegorical interpretation because a spiritual meaning beyond the apparent meaning of the text is sought. Unlike the allegorical approach which either disregards the reality of history or sees the historical events as quite irrelevant in view of the deeper truth that the allegorical method reveals, the typological method affirms that there is a solid historical reality described in the story. Two levels of meaning are attached to the story. The events recounted in the Song involve Solomon's relationship with a girl whom he married. The events described, however, are a type or illustration of the relationship between God/Christ and His people (Israel, the church, or the individual believer) and teach important truths about that spiritual relationship. Christian interpreters see Solomon as a type or figure illustrative of Christ and the bride of the church and find parallels between Solomon and his bride and Christ and His church, which range from quite general correspondences to detailed similarities that differ little from those produced by the allegorical method.

The fact that Scripture often describes the relationship between God and His people in terms of the relationship between a husband and wife, and the fact that Psalm 45, a song of love (or a wedding song as NIV translates it) apparently in praise of the king on his wedding day, is applied to the Messiah by the author of Hebrews (Heb. 1:8)[5] does give support to the idea that this story about love between two people is supposed to remind us of that higher love that God has for His people. Few Evangelicals would deny this point, but many remain skeptical about the typological view, largely because the method is often applied in a way that obscures what seems to many to be the primary purpose for which the book was written. The Song is never applied to the Messiah in the New Testament—it is not quoted at all there—and there is no indication in the text of the Song to suggest that it is describing anything other than human love.

---

[5] Carr (TOTC, pp. 26–32) has pointed out basic differences between the Song and Psalm 45 that undermine the significance of this comparison to support the legitimacy of the typical or allegorical interpretation of the Song.

This does not preclude the possibility that a beautiful example of human love may legitimately turn our thoughts to the even higher love of God for His people, but it does raise serious questions as to whether there are two levels of meaning that can be legitimately found throughout the Song. Few would object to an application of the typological method that finds only the most general correspondences between the human love described in the book and God's love for His people. There are serious dangers, however, in those applications of the typological method that seek correspondences between the two levels of meaning in such detail that the natural meaning of the text, which exegetically must be primary, is lost. The method, in its application, is often little different than the allegorical method, and imaginative but subjectively-determined interpretations are presented as if they were the primary meaning of the inspired text, while what appears to be the primary meaning of the text is largely ignored.

C. Mythology

The economy throughout the ancient Near East was largely based on farming and the raising of small cattle or sheep and goats. The people realized that their economic well-being depended on abundant production, and they realized that success in these areas was contingent on natural forces over which they had limited control. Their religion offered them a means by which they could appease the gods and thus hopefully ensure optimum conditions in their fields, flocks, and households. Their religious ritual used magic as a means of influencing the gods and making sure that they were favorably disposed toward those who worshiped them. The fertility religions made use of sympathetic magic in which worshipers had sexual relations with cult priests and priestesses to stimulate the gods to cause their fields and flocks to produce abundantly.

Scholars have pieced together certain mythological stories, apparently based on the yearly cycle of nature, that seem to involve a god who died in the fall, who was pursued into the netherworld by his lover, and was resurrected in the spring. This myth was presumably celebrated in the cult with two people assuming the roles of the god Tammuz and the goddess Ishtar (or the corresponding gods worshiped in a particular locality) and then ritually acting out the story of the myth. It has been suggested by some that the Song of Songs had its origins in the fertility cult that flourished in Canaan before the arrival of the Hebrews and continued to exist there despite the efforts of the priests and prophets to eradicate it. (Ezekiel 8:14 suggests that a form of the fertility cult involving Tammuz existed in Jerusalem prior to the Babylonian Exile.) Marvin Pope[6] has recently advocated a modification of this view and his commentary will, no doubt, do much to popularize the view. Pope suggests that the material in the Song may have once been associated with an ancient cultic funeral feast. He notes that the power of love over death is affirmed in 8:6, and he suggests that the book makes the powerful statement that, in the face of death, love is the only power that can cope with death.

It is by no means certain that there was an ancient cult ritual that celebrated the god's release from the grip of death through the help of a goddess. Even if scholars are correct in their reconstruction of these myths and the ritual (fertility or funeral) associated with them, it seems quite unlikely that the Song of Songs could have had its origins there. Even apart from the question of the inspiration of Scripture, which seems to decisively preclude the possibility of this kind of origin for the Song, many objections to these theories can be raised. Except for a few expressions in the book that could possibly be seen as heavily veiled allusions to something cultic (All of these are much more plausibly understood in totally non-cultic terms.), there is nothing to suggest such a connection. There is no reference to God (or gods) or to anything religious (one of the peculiar features of the book), and the book is entirely lacking in religious or cultic terminology. The prophets strongly denounced pagan religion and idolatry and saw this as the reason for God's judgment on Judah. Prophets, like Ezekiel, recognized the presence of fertility religion in Jerusalem but condemned it as an abomination. After the Exile, idolatry seems to have been essentially eliminated as a major religious problem among the

---

[6] Pope, AB, pp. 210–19.

Jews, and idolatry was seen as totally repugnant to both the people and the religious leaders. The idea that literature originally associated with the pagan fertility or funeral cult could have lost those associations, become accepted by orthodox religion, and finally could have been accepted as Scripture is extremely unlikely.[7]

D. Literal

The literal (or plain sense) interpretation of the Song takes the Song at face value and concludes that it is a book of love poetry. The literal interpretation recognizes that the book makes extensive use of symbolic and figurative language, but it recognizes this as an integral part of the poetic description of the relationship between a man and a woman who are in love. Even though most modern interpreters agree that the literal interpretation of the Song is the correct one, there remain many different opinions about such matters as the literary form of the book, the story told in the book, the purpose of the book, etc.

1. The Literary Form of the Book

a. **Drama.** This view, which has largely been abandoned by commentators today, suggests that the Song is in the literary form of a drama. Stage directions are entirely lacking in the text and must be supplied by the reader. The individual sections in the book, which again must be identified by the reader, are viewed as different scenes in the drama. The identity of each speaker in the various dialogues must be determined, and this is simplified somewhat by the fact that Hebrew uses different forms when referring to men and women. The sections spoken by a group of people (perhaps the daughters of Jerusalem and usually made clear by the use of Hebrew plural forms) are seen as indicative of something like the chorus in dramatic presentations.

Though some have suggested that the book was written to be acted out (sometimes in connection with the mythological cult theory mentioned above), this seems quite unlikely for several reasons. The subject matter of the book seems to

---

[7]A detailed analysis and refutation of the cultic view can be found in Jack Deere, "Meaning of the Song," pp. 12–49.

preclude this. In addition, there is little evidence for the existence of drama among the Semites and no evidence for it among the Jews. According to Oesterly, "To the Jews of old, dramatic performances were held in horror because they were regarded as heathenish and irreligious."[8] It is highly unlikely that a drama like this would have been accepted by Jewish religious leaders, and the possibility that it could have been accepted into the canon seems even more remote. Many who have accepted this view have suggested that the Song was never intended to be acted out, rather it was written as a kind of dramatic reading. Advocates of the dramatic view are not agreed as to the story told in the book, although all would agree that there is a unified story.

Even though there are few today who accept the view that the literary form of the Song is drama,[9] the necessity for determining some kind of "stage directions" (at least to the extent of identifying the various speakers) is recognized by all who conclude that there is a continuous story in the book. This is reflected in the suggested identification of speakers that is found in the margin of many translations of the Bible, including some of the oldest Greek translations.

b. Semitic Love Poetry. Even a casual reading of Song of Songs in Hebrew makes it clear that the book is written in poetry, and this is reflected in the format of most modern translations. When the Song is compared with love poetry from elsewhere in the ancient Near East,[10] it becomes clear that there are significant similarities in themes, in the literary figures that are used, in the kind of language, and in other respects as well. The lovers frequently refer to one another as "brother" and "sister," and royal terminology is used in describing one another. Detailed descriptions of the beauty of the lovers' physical features are frequently found in this kind of poetry, and the descriptions are often couched in images taken from the world of nature. The lovers frankly express their love for one another as well as their desire to express that love in an intimate

---

[8] Cited by Rowley, "Interpretation," p. 205, n. 2.

[9] Note the brief but significant objections of Carr, TOTC, pp. 32–34.

[10] See the summary discussion by Carr, TOTC, pp. 37–41 and the references cited there.

way. Mention is made of obstacles that complicate the relationship, such as their inability to be alone together, family members who try to thwart the relationship, separations beyond their control, and the like. A comparison of the Song with love poetry in general makes it clear that the Song contains many features typical of love poetry from all over the world and from every period of history.[11]

It seems probable that Song of Songs is simply an inspired example of Hebrew love poetry. This clearly is the plain-sense meaning of the text. The primary reason that this conclusion has been resisted is that this is felt to be a theme unworthy of inclusion in Holy Scripture. This question will be considered later when the purpose of the book is discussed.

For Further Study

1. What is the difference between allegory and typology?

2. Read Psalm 45. How is it similar to Song of Songs? How is it different?

3. Look up "Baal," "Asherah," and "Canaanite Religion" in a Bible dictionary or encyclopedia.

---

[11] Enough examples to establish the point are given by Pope, AB, pp. 54–89.

Chapter 3

The Story of the Song

As has been previously noted, there is little in the poetic narrative of the Song that can be clearly recognized as the plot of the book, and every attempt to construct a unified and coherent story from the poems requires a considerable amount of reading between the lines. This fact has given rise to three primary views about the story presented in the book.

A. Anthology

This view maintains that there is no coherent story contained in the book; rather, it is simply a collection of poems, similar to that found in the Book of Psalms but about the subject of human love. The similarities in language, theme, etc. among the poems are said to be simply characteristic of love poetry from a common cultural source.

There are, though, in the eight chapters that make up the book several expressions that are repeated in a way that suggests the unity of the book. The daughters of Jerusalem appear in the book a number of times (1:5; 2:7; 3:5, 11 [daughters of Zion]; 5:8, 16; 8:4 and they are mentioned again in 3:10) and on three different occasions they are urged by the girl (the beloved) not to arouse love before it is appropriate (2:7; 3:5 and 8:4). The term "my lover" is used by the girl thirty-one times in the book; the girl is referred to as "my darling" nine times, as "my bride" six times, and as "my sister" seven times. Solomon is mentioned seven times, and the king is mentioned five times. These repetitions combined with what some see as a progression in the relationship described in the Song suggests that the Song is a unity and does tell some sort of coherent story. Landy concludes that the Song "is a unity . . . , in part because of its thematic coherence, . . . ; and in part because of the reappearance of the same elements in diverse contexts, as leitmotivs, refrains, episodes that repeat each other with variations."[1]

Certainly, the indications of unity are much different than would be expected in a prose narrative, and the development of the plot is far less obvious as well. This is to some degree the result of the poetic medium of the Song. Poetry is not the normal vehicle for telling a story; it is the language of emotion and feeling rather than instruction. These poems are intended to express the intense delight and desire that the lovers have for each other rather than the logical details of their developing relationship. The story in the Song is told through a sequence of poetic pictures that Glickman compares to a series of snapshots in an album,[2] and in a way typical of a lyric ballad, the Song moves from scene to scene without filling in the connecting links. Reconstructing the story is further complicated by the fact that the "pictures" do not necessarily appear in chronological or logical order. Thus, while there are some indications of the unity of the book and the likelihood of a coherent story underlying the book, the poetry does not provide enough clear data to determine exactly what that story is.

B. The Three-Character View (Shepherd Hypothesis)

Apart from the idea that the Solomon who appears in this book is a kind of fictionalized ideal figure, those who conclude that the book is a unity generally understand the references to Solomon as connecting this well-known king to the events described in the Song. Many have resisted the apparently obvious conclusion that Solomon is the lover in the Song on the grounds that Solomon, notorious for his large harem (1 Kings 11:3) and his ungodly marriage alliances (1 Kings 11:1–6) could not be an example of ideal or virtuous human love. Since it is

---

[1] Francis Landy, "Beauty and the Enigma: An Inquiry into Some Interrelated Episodes of the Song of Songs," *Journal for the Study of the Old Testament*, 17 (1980), p. 94, n. 9.

[2] S. Craig Glickman, *A Song for Lovers* (Downers Grove, Illinois: InterVarsity Press, 1976), pp. 28–29.

unthinkable that this inspired book would praise the purely physical and erotic, an alternative view known as the Shepherd Hypothesis has been suggested.[3]

According to this view, Solomon saw a beautiful young girl in a rural region of northern Israel while he was traveling in that area. He was struck by her beauty and ordered her brought to Jerusalem where he meant to add her to his harem. Solomon wooed her as he praised her beauty and told her of his desire for her; the women of the court told her about the splendid life she would enjoy as Solomon's wife. The girl, however, loved a shepherd boy from her home region so she resisted all the urgings of the women who praised Solomon and all the courting and enticements of Solomon. She resisted his advances and finally Solomon, aware that his efforts to win the girl's love had not succeeded, reluctantly allowed the girl to return to the shepherd whom she loved.

It is recognized by most that 8:6–7 constitutes a sort of climax to the book and contains one of the most important points made by the book. Verse 7 says, "Many waters cannot quench love: rivers cannot wash it away. If one were to give all the wealth of his house for love, it would be utterly scorned." It is clear that the Shepherd Hypothesis fits well with the point made by this verse. The love of the girl for her shepherd could not be quenched by the difficulty of the separation that resulted from her being taken by the king to Jerusalem. Nor could it be quenched by the offer of great wealth and honor that would come to the girl as one of Solomon's wives. It has been suggested that the political situation following the death of Solomon could well account for the book's being written and circulated in the North. The book, in this view, was something of a satire about Solomon and the conditions of his reign, and it described one occasion when this king whose money and power allowed him to have essentially everything that he wanted was thwarted by a simple country maid from the North. The people in the North would have taken great delight in a story like this about the "great" king whose harsh policies contributed sig-

[3]See, for example, F. Godet, "The Interpretation of the Song of Songs," reprinted in Walter Kaiser, ed., *Classical Evangelical Essays in Old Testament Interpretation* (Grand Rapids, Michigan: Baker Book House, 1972), pp. 151–75.

nificantly to the division of the kingdom immediately after his death.

There are some very appealing features about this view. It clearly solves the problem created if Solomon is the hero of the story and is the model for love between a man and woman. The important point made by 8:6–7 is well supported and illustrated by the story related in the book. The political situation in Israel and Judah creates a suitable environment for the writing and circulation of the story. Despite the strong support that can be presented for this view, it is not without its problems. A casual reading of the book would never lead one to suspect that this is the correct interpretation of the book. The Shepherd Hypothesis was suggested precisely because the obvious and plain-sense interpretation of the story with Solomon as the lover is problematic because of his notorious reputation.

There are times when an interpreter must opt for something other than the apparent meaning of a word or verse to harmonize it with other verses or passages that define the total context of the passage. It is not so much the fact that this must be done when one accepts the Shepherd Hypothesis; it is rather the extent to which it must be done that poses serious problems for the view. For example, in 1:15–2:3 there is a dialogue between the lover and the beloved in which the compliments of the lover are returned to him in almost identical words. The Shepherd Hypothesis argues that the words of the beloved are, in fact, not directed to Solomon, who praised the girl, but are instead directed to her absent lover, and a similar procedure is required throughout the book. It is generally agreed that 4:12–5:1 describes the physical consummation of the relationship between the man and the woman. The Shepherd Hypothesis sees this as something that Solomon tried to force on the girl (though her words in 4:16 sound like her invitation for this to occur) or as something that she saw in a dream (see 5:2) as happening between her and her absent lover or as something that actually happened after Solomon allowed her to return home. In other instances as well, it is suggested that the incidents related are not romantic encounters between the girl and Solomon, but rather the girl's dream in which she envisions an encounter with her absent shepherd.[4]

This view has obvious appeal, but its major weakness appears to be exegetical. This view requires, in more than one instance, an unnatural reading of the text; at times it requires that speeches apparently coming from one individual be parceled out between the shepherd and Solomon and it requires that words apparently directed to one person actually be directed to a character whose actual existence in the story is at best only implied. Certainly, this view is possible, but because so much has to be read between the lines and because so many apparently subjective judgments are required to determine where the shepherd appears, to whom the girl's remarks are directed, which incidents are dreams and which are actual events, etc., the view does not really engender confidence that the suggested interpretations are either exegetically necessary or even probable.

C. The Two-Character View

This view recognizes Solomon as the lover in the Song and sees in it a description of his relationship with a young country girl from the northern part of Israel. The maiden is wooed and won by King Solomon, and the Song describes the excitement and beauty of their love for each other. Apart from the problem posed by Solomon's notorious reputation, this view is clearly the simplest and the most straightforward interpretation of the Song.

While this problem is not an insignificant one for the two-character view, several solutions have been suggested which, while not totally convincing, are sufficiently plausible to make this the preferable view. It has been suggested that this book describes Solomon's relationship with the girl whom he truly loved in contrast with the politically-expedient marriages that he entered into. Others have suggested that the relatively small harem (at least in comparison with the numbers noted in 1 Kings 11:3) mentioned in 6:8 was something inherited from

---

[4]Examples of how these matters are handled can be seen in the article by Godet (see n. 21) and in the discussion by G. Hassel Bullock, *An Introduction to the Poetic Books of the Old Testament* (Chicago: Moody Press, 1972), pp. 242–54.

his father David rather than a harem that he possessed sexually. An ancient Jewish tradition, still followed by many advocates of this view, suggested that the Song was written when Solomon was young. As Glickman suggests,

"One might imagine that so lofty a love as Canticles depicts, if taken away by death, might affect an empty and fruitless search to replace it with the many wives Solomon later possessed. His writing of proverbs did not later prevent his unwise behavior. So perhaps it is only consistent with the character of Solomon that the faithful love of Canticles would not prevent his later promiscuous affairs."[5]

In the present author's opinion, the most plausible explanation seems to be the suggestion that this story is not something that actually happened, but rather a kind of illustrative example written by Solomon to describe the ideal relationship between a man and woman. Just as Solomon was noted for his proverbial lore—much of which he did not personally apply—so his great wisdom (empowered and illuminated by the Spirit of God) enabled him to understand and describe a relationship that he never experienced. Thus, the ideal that Solomon describes here stands in strong contrast to his own failures in marriage. As has been previously noted, this suggested solution to the problem posed by Solomon's character by no means solves every problem; it is, like many other proposed solutions to the problems raised by this little book, only a plausible one. This solution does pave the way for the interpretation of the book that is the most straightforward exegetically, and this seems preferable to the other suggestions proposed by interpreters.

For Further Study

1. What is the difference between the anthology view, the three-character view, and the two-character view?

2. How do verses like 8:7 offer support for the three-character view? Does the verse create problems for the two-character view?

3. Read 1:15–2:3 and 4:1–5:1. Does the three-character view seem plausible in view of the apparent meaning of these sections?

---

[5]Glickman, *Song for Lovers*, p. 181.

Chapter 4

The Purpose of the Song

There is in this book no explicitly religious theme or reference to God; major religious terminology is missing as well. The primary basis for determining the purpose for which the book was written is the content of the book and its present canonical context (Certainly what was seen as purely erotic poetry would not have been accepted into the canon.). Those who conclude that the Song is to be interpreted allegorically or typologically will, of course, understand the Song to be teaching important truths about the relationship between God and His people. Those who conclude that the Song is to be interpreted literally will normally see the purpose of the book in one of three ways.

A. Wedding Song

Several scholars during the last half of the nineteenth century pointed out similarities between Syrian wedding poetry and the poetry in Song of Solomon; parallels were also suggested between the Song and wedding practices observed in Syria.[1] These studies led to the suggestion that the Song is a collection of poems sung in connection with the wedding ceremonies of the people. Support for this view is found in the similarity between the poems in the Song praising the beauty of

---

[1]Specific references can be found in Rowley, "Interpretation," pp. 209–12 and Pope, AB, pp. 141–45. An English translation of the important study by Wetzstein can be found in F. Delitzsch, *Commentary on the Song of Songs*, tr. by M. G. Easton (Grand Rapids, Michigan: Wm. B. Eerdmans Publishing Co., 1950), pp. 162–76.

the lovers and an Arabic song called a *wasaf* praising the bride and bridegroom at weddings (and on other occasions as well). Gordis says, "That the praise of the bride on her wedding day was a regular feature of Jewish weddings in Second Temple days, and that these songs of praise were a technical art . . . is clear from an ancient Talmudic tradition."[2]

It has been suggested that the Song can be divided into sections that correspond to the seven-day wedding celebration observed among the Arabs and for which there are clear references in Jewish tradition as well.[3] The reference to the bride and groom in Syrian weddings as king and queen prompted the suggestion that the same thing is happening in the Song as the groom becomes Solomon and the bride Shulamite (6;13), supposed by some to be a feminine form of the name Solomon. The mention of Solomon's crown in 3:11 may have to do only with the fact that he was the king, though the verse seems to specifically relate it to his wedding. As Gordis has noted, "Crowns were worn even by ordinary grooms and brides, until the defeats sustained in the war against Rome in 70, when they were abandoned as a sign of mourning."[4]

Certainly, there is much in the Song that can be appropriately applied to weddings and no doubt this has been done to some extent wherever the Song was known. It seems likely as well that various elements in the Song were influenced, if not determined, by the wedding traditions that existed when the Song was written, particularly since 3:11 clearly connects the material with a wedding day. There are, though, several things that make it unlikely that the entire Song is a kind of wedding ritual. It is, first of all, very difficult to suppose that nineteenth-century Syrian wedding customs accurately reflect Jewish practices during the biblical period, given the great differences in both time and culture. Subsequent studies of Arab wedding customs have revealed sufficient differences from those initially suggested, and this raises further questions about the possibility of establishing a credible link between modern Arab practice

---

[2] Robert Gordis, *The Song of Songs and Lamentations*, (New York: KTAV Publishing House, revised and augmented 1974), p. 17.

[3] Ibid., p. 17, n. 67.

[4] Ibid., p. 86.

and the biblical world on this point. There are sections of the Song that appear to have nothing to do with marriage; there are other sections that, as Carr suggests, "may suggest some sort of celebration sequence which the Song mirrors."[5] Without question, this idea has contributed significantly to our understanding of the Song; however, it does not appear to provide a comprehensive scheme for understanding the purpose for which the Song was written.

B. Didactic

Many interpreters of the Song suppose that the praise of human love would not be a sufficient basis for this book's inclusion into the canon of inspired Scripture, and they look for some teaching or didactic purpose beyond the celebration of human love. Those who interpret the book allegorically or typologically find in the book profound teachings about the relationship between God and His people. Those who follow the Shepherd Hypothesis find in the book an example of great virtue in that the girl's love for her shepherd was not set aside for the wealth and glory that Solomon offered the girl if she would become his wife. Some have tried to find in the Song a social or ethical message about a proper view of women and/or marriage.

It is clear that some very important lessons about the relationship between a man and a woman can be learned from the examples described in this book. It seems likely, though, that the primary purpose of the book is something different than the overt teaching of these principles.

C. Celebration or Praise of Human Love

This view suggests that the primary purpose of Song of Songs was to praise or celebrate human love as a gift from God and that no primary purpose beyond that needs to be sought. This suggestion is fully consistent with what appears to be the straightforward meaning of the text and is the view held by the majority of commentators today, both Evangelical and otherwise. The major objection to this view of the book comes from

[5]Carr, TOTC, p. 53.

the fact that prior to the last couple of centuries, it had been consistently rejected as a valid view by believers who felt that human love was not a topic of sufficient worth and virtue to merit celebration in Scripture. The comment of Hengstenberg, at a time when some were advocating the literal interpretation, is characteristic of the feeling of most earlier interpreters. He said, "The literal interpretation of this Book gained its honors in the age of Rationalism, when the Church was degraded to its lowest level, and when it was bare and void of sound ecclesiastical judgment, and of holy taste and tact."[6]

It must be recognized that the view of human sexuality of past generations was very different from the view of our generation, and this difference goes far in explaining why modern interpreters are willing to accept an interpretation of this book that previous generations of believers categorically rejected as carnal. An awareness of how cultural values have influenced (or perhaps more accurately determined) the interpretation of this book is important. It is also important to be aware of the various influences that affect our values and attitudes in these areas, and it is impossible to avoid the conclusion that television, movies, and literature of many kinds have significantly changed society's values about sexual morality and ethics. Many things that were considered to be wrong or socially unacceptable a generation ago are now seen as appropriate by most people in the Evangelical church.

It is clear that cultural values do influence our interpretation of Scripture; it is clear as well that the values and attitudes of our culture regarding human sexuality have changed and make us more open to an interpretation of Song of Songs that had been vigorously rejected by virtually every biblical scholar for well over fifteen hundred years. An awareness of the history of interpretation of the Song, coupled with Paul's warning in Romans 12:2 against letting the world determine our values as believers, must stand as a major consideration for the modern interpreter of Song of Solomon. At the same time, the teaching of Scripture must stand as the ultimate authority and judge on any issue and the biblical understanding of sex must be the

---

[6]Cited by Pope, AB, p. 126.

standard by which the various cultural perspectives are evaluated.

According to Genesis 2, after God put the man in the garden He had made for him, He indicated that it was not good for the man to be alone and that a suitable helper was needed for the man. First, a suitable helper was sought among the animals that God had made, but none was found there. One reason for this is apparent from the creation account in Genesis 1, where the image of God in man sets him apart from everything else that God made. Thus, the man had to have another human being made in the image of God for God's purposes in the "suitable helper" to be realized. When God made the suitable helper for the man, however, He made a female human being; thus, it is evident that the ideal human relationship that was intended here included a sexual relationship. Certainly, a major reason for this is the necessity for reproduction, which is quite clear from the command to "Be fruitful and increase in number; fill the earth," that God gave to the people he had created in 1:28. The "one flesh" relationship that prompts a man to leave his parents and cleave to his wife (Gen. 2:24), while encompassing every aspect of their relationship, obviously includes the sexual.

It is the wisdom literature, of which Song of Songs is a part, that provides the closest thing to an extended commentary on this relationship between man and woman.[7] Wisdom to the Hebrews involved not so much thinking profound thoughts as practical skills for living. Therefore, wisdom was the ability to succeed, and the search for wisdom proceeded out of several important presuppositions. Wisdom recognized that God created everything and that there is an order and stability established by the creative and sustaining power of God. Because man is created in the image of God, he has the faculties and insight to study his world and society and to identify the patterns and principles that operate there and contribute to man's success in

---

[7]It is perhaps worth noting that in Gen. 5:1–2 it is the male and female together, no doubt in this "one flesh" relationship, that God called "Adam" or "man." This not only affirms the importance of the relationship; it even suggests that it is in this relationship that male and female are complete.

the world that God made.[8] Much of the material contained in Proverbs, Job, and Ecclesiastes had its origins in this search for the principles that contribute to man's success in the world and society; the importance of this search is clearly affirmed by the fact that God made many of these principles part of His inspired Word to us.

The relationship between a man and a woman is one of the basic components of human experience and this was a subject of interest to the wisdom writers. The mystery and wonder of the relationship is noted in Proverbs 30:18–19: One of the things too wonderful to understand is "the way of the man with a maiden." The positive potential of this relationship is assured by the design and creation of God as is indicated in Genesis 2:18–25; the Fall and subsequent judgment (Gen. 3:16) introduce a significant disruption into the relationship, and both the positive and negative possibilities of the relationship are recognized throughout the Book of Proverbs. Proverbs gives considerable attention to warnings about the wrong kind of relationships, and these include clear indications of the proper moral context in which the relationship between a man and a woman is to be developed. Proverbs 5–7 contain numerous warnings about becoming involved with the "strange" woman (i.e., the adulteress or prostitute). Proverbs 5:15–20 makes it clear that a married couple's delight and enjoyment of the sexual aspect of their relationship is both proper and an important antidote to the problem posed by the "strange" woman, and it affirms this in language every bit as explicit as the language of Song of Songs. Given the context in which this occurs, there can be no question that it refers to the sexual relationship between a man and his wife. It affirms this as a proper and positive part of their relationship, even if it does so in bold language that creates discomfort for some even in the twentieth-century church.

As the author of Ecclesiastes seeks the key to the meaning of life, he considers a number of possibilities that lead to the conclusion that life is vanity. As he points out the uncertainties of life and the many aspects of life over which man, despite what

---

[8]For a general discussion and references see Edward M. Curtis, "Old Testament Wisdom: A Model for Faith-Learning Integration," *Christian Scholar's Review*, xv (1986), pp. 213–27.

he does, has little control, he again and again concludes that the proper way to live is to fear God and to eat, drink, and to enjoy life with your wife whom you love (e.g., Eccl. 9:7–9); it seems clear that the inspired writer wants his readers to follow this advice.[9] Underlying his advice, as well as the perspective of Song of Songs, is a concept of man that is very different than the view of certain Greek philosophers who had a significant impact on early Christian theology. The Greeks supposed that since the gods were good and since they were spirit, the material must be evil. They concluded that man's body, since it is material, must be evil and that the truly significant part of man is his immaterial aspect. This idea was adopted into theology and led to the denigration of the physical part of man and to the idea that the physical desires of man are evil (or at least significantly inferior to the immaterial or spiritual aspect of man), and this idea found its most radical expression in monasticism. The supposition that man's physical aspect and the desires associated with it are inferior, if not overtly evil, precludes the possibility of understanding the Song of Songs as a praise of human love. The Bible, though, sees man's body as created by God and as an essential and significant aspect of man. Man's physical desires are seen as a gift of God for man to use and enjoy. Thus, the understanding of the Song as praise to human love seems to be entirely consistent with the biblical perspective.

Among the criticisms leveled by past generations against the kind of interpretation we are suggesting is the fact that this reduces the poetry to the level of any other purely erotic poetry. Rabbi Akiba, in the first century AD, condemned those who sang this as a common song at banquets. Calvin opposed a colleague in part because "He considers that it [the Song] is a lascivious and obscene poem in which Solomon has described his shameless love affairs."[10] Rowley also cites a 1651 Westminster Assembly book of notes about the Bible that speaks of people who "received it [the Song] as an hot carnal pamphlet, formed

---

[9] In support of this conclusion see J. Stafford Wright, "The Interpretation of Ecclesiastes," in *Classical Evangelical Essays in Old Testament Interpretation*, ed. by Walter Kaiser (Grand Rapids, Michigan: Baker Book House, 1972), pp. 133–50.

[10] Cited by Rowley, "Interpretation," p. 207, n. 1.

by some loose Apollo or Cupid."[11] We have already suggested that the Bible affirms human sexuality and its proper expression as a gift of God that is to be received and enjoyed by the creatures that He made. The Bible also makes it clear that there are certain parameters within which these good gifts of the Creation are to be used, and marriage represents the relationship within which the gift of sex is to be enjoyed.

The Song does not explicitly state that marriage is the context for sexual intimacy, though this is clearly suggested by the fact that the scene in which the sexual consummation of the relationship occurs (4:1–5:1) takes place after one passage that does mention King Solomon's wedding day (3:11). It is suggested by the references to the girl as "bride" (4:8–12; 5:1) after 3:11 as well. This exploration of the male-female relationship is found in the wisdom literature and the search for true wisdom was constrained and guided by the fear of the Lord (Prov. 1:7; 9:10). Biblical wisdom presupposes God's covenant with Israel and that law establishes certain limits for wise behavior. The Song celebrates the human capacity to love as ordered by the Creator, and the full and intimate expression of love presupposes a relationship that involves the commitment of marriage. The fact of marriage is not, however, the focus of the Song; rather the delight of the two lovers in one another, their praise of the other's beauty, and their desire for one another is the emphasis throughout the poetry.

It is the fact that the Song celebrates love between a man and a woman in marriage that makes what would otherwise be erotic poetry into a proper celebration of pure love in its manifold expressions. The Song is a commentary on the statement of Genesis 2:24 and explores and celebrates what the "one flesh relationship" was intended by God to involve.

We are suggesting then that the Song of Songs is a celebration of love between a man and a woman. Their capacity to love is accepted as a beautiful gift of God to His creation and the depth, passion, power, and intensity of love are celebrated in these poems. We are suggesting that these poems, which capture isolated incidents in the experience of the lovers, are

[11] Ibid., p. 233, n. 3.

arranged in a way that traces the development of the relationship to its consummation in marriage and sees the physical and sexual expression of love as appropriate only in the context of that commitment. Some of the poems describe experiences that test and threaten this relationship and then narrate the lovers' struggles and victory over these obstacles.

The message of the Song comes to us in a generation where the spirit of the age allows us to accept the book as it was originally meant to be understood, as a celebration of human love. At the same time, the preoccupation of our society with the purely physical aspects of human sexuality, its glorification of sex, and its view of sex as a self-centered and self-serving means of self-gratification has produced a distorted and bizarre perspective that desperately needs the correcting message of Song of Songs and the rest of Scripture as well. The passion of sex is evident throughout our society, but not the kind of exclusive commitment that is presupposed in the Song and demanded throughout Scripture. The delight with and appreciation for one another that characterizes the Song is largely absent in our culture; the moral values that prescribe and limit the exercise of God's gift of sex to humanity are not only ignored, they are overtly denied by much of our society. The believing community needs to understand the mystery of the love relationship between a man and a woman as a beautiful and wonderful gift of God.

The kind of appreciation and excitement for one another that is depicted in the Song needs to be cultivated and developed as the relationship changes and matures beyond the initial years of marriage. Our society needs to hear the Song's message about the kind of exclusive and deep commitment to one another that works hard to overcome the difficulties and problems that inevitably come into every relationship. The Song describes an important aspect of the relationship that is one of God's best gifts to human beings made in His image; it is a message that will contribute much to making our marriages what God wants them to be. It is a message that will help us to glorify God in this important relationship by making our marriages examples of the kind of love that Christ has for the church.

As many have pointed out, the celebration of human love in

the Song cannot help but remind us of the even higher and purer love that God has for His people and perhaps this cannot be expressed better than in the often quoted words of E. J. Young.

> The Song does celebrate the dignity and purity of human love. This is a fact that has not always been sufficiently stressed. The Song, therefore, is didactic and moral in its purpose. It comes to us in this world of sin, where lust and passion are on every hand, where fierce temptations assail us and try to turn us aside from the God-given standard of marriage. And it reminds us, in particularly beautiful fashion, how pure and noble true love is. This, however, does not exhaust the purpose of the book. Not only does it speak of the purity of human love, but by its very inclusion in the Canon, it reminds us of a love that is purer than our own.[12]

For Further Study

1. How do passages like Genesis 2:18–25, Proverbs 5:15–19, 1 Corinthians 7:1–7, Ephesians 5:22–33, and 1 Peter 3:1–7 relate to the question of the purpose for which the Song was written?

2. Read Deuteronomy 2:13–29; Exodus 22:16–17; Romans 13:13–14; 1 Corinthians 6:15–20; Ephesians 5:3–6; 1 Thessalonians 4:2–7. What relevance do these and similar passages have for the question of whether the sexual activity described in the Song takes place outside the parameters of marriage?

---

[12] E. J. Young, *An Introduction to the Old Testament* (2nd ed.; Grand Rapids, Michigan: William B. Eerdmans Publishing Company, 1960), p. 354.

Chapter 5

Hebrew Poetry and the Language of the Song

The Song is written in poetry and thus reflects many of the characteristics of poetry, including those somewhat peculiar to Semitic poetry. Hebrew poetry is not characterized by such things as the rhyme or the rigid metrical patterns that are often typical of Western poetry. The basic characteristic of Hebrew poetry is something called parallelism. This involves the statement of an idea in one line and a restatement of that same basic thought in the second line. Often this takes a form called synonymous parallelism in which the second line simply repeats the idea of the first line in different words, and there are many examples of this in the Song. For example,

> Arise, come, my darling;
> My beautiful one, come with me (2:13).

or

> You are a garden locked up, my sister, my bride;
> You are a spring enclosed, a sealed fountain (4:12).

An important variation of synonymous parallelism is called climactic parallelism, in which the second line takes words from the first and develops the idea further than was done in the first line. For example:

> All night on my bed I looked for the one my heart
>   loves;
> I looked for him but I did not find him (3:1).

You are a garden fountain,
a well of flowing water streaming down from Lebanon
    (4:15).

A third kind of parallelism that is common in the Song is called synthetic parallelism in which the second line develops the thought of the first, but without repeating any of the words from the first line. Several examples of synthetic parallelism are found in the lover's description of his beloved, developed further in each succeeding line. For example,

Your teeth are like a flock of sheep just shorn,
    coming up from the washing.
        Each has its twin;
    not one of them is alone. (4:2)

This repetition, which is an integral part of the parallelism, reinforces the ideas and gives the poetry a power that is sometimes lacking in other kinds of poetry. Allen has likened parallelism to a stereophonic music system: Two slightly different but complementary sounds come from each speaker and blend together to make the total sound.[1] The parallel poetic lines *together* make a single point, and this is an important point to remember when interpreting Hebrew poetry. Song of Solomon 5:3 says,

I have taken off my robe—must I put it on again?
I have washed my feet—must I soil them again?

The two halves of the verse are synonymously parallel; they describe quite different acts, but there is a common denominator in the two actions that is the focus of the poet's interest. The two lines together make the single point that the girl had already retired for the night and was reluctant to be disturbed.

In addition to a poetic form that the Song shares with other Hebrew (and Semitic) poetry, the language of the Song has much in common with poetry in general. Poetry is normally not the literary form that is used to communicate information; rather, poetry is intended to communicate feeling and experience. The language of the Song is meant to reproduce in the

---

[1] Ronald B. Allen, *Praise! A Matter of Life and Breath* (Nashville, Tennessee: Thomas Nelson Publishers, 1978), p. 51.

reader the experiences of the two lovers; it is supposed to make the reader feel their delight and excitement with each other.

Metaphors, often taken from the realm of nature, are frequently used to accomplish this. There must be an objective point of contact between the figure (e.g., a dove or a flock of goats) and that which it describes (her eyes or her hair). There will normally be some common point in the comparison that makes the comparison appropriate, and one would not expect to find her teeth compared with a piece of coal; rather, they are compared with newly washed sheep. Thus, his body has something in common with polished ivory (perhaps smoothness or color), as do his legs with pillars of marble (perhaps color or strength or the appearance of the rippling muscles).

The power of the metaphor lies in the feelings that the figure evokes in the hearer because of the associations that he makes between the two elements in the comparison, and often what the language denotes is less important than the feelings and emotions that it evokes in the reader. The communicative power of phrases like "Chestnuts roasting on an open fire, Jack Frost nipping at your nose" goes beyond what it denotes to the emotions that those words evoke from the experiences of the hearer. The same is true of the compliments that the two lovers have for one another.

Strongly positive compliments are communicated through these figures and thus one would not expect negative connotations to be conveyed through the comparisons (One would not compare her eyes to a cess pool.). Often, there are elements in the comparisons that are culturally conditioned and our great distance from the world and culture of the Song makes it difficult to understand and appreciate some of the figures used in this poetry. The comparisons with nature are sometimes far different than we would choose and reflect cultural values and ideas of beauty that are different from ours. Most women today would not be pleased by a comment such as the one found in 4:4, "Your neck is like the tower of David, built with elegance; on it hang a thousand shields." Nor would they take the words "Your hair is like a flock of goats descending from Mount Gilead" (4:4) as an affectionate and endearing remark. These expressions are meant to describe the physical beauty of the girl (or the man), and they do have an intellectual content, even if sometimes our differing standards of beauty make it difficult to appreciate the significance of the description (e.g., "your nose is like the tower of Lebanon looking toward Damascus" [7:4]). Not only do the metaphors move beyond the physical description to communicate an emotional message, they sometimes have a symbolic aspect as well.

As Gordis has pointed out, the Song, like other love poetry, often uses symbolic language to express nuances beyond the power of exact definition. He says,

> When, for example, the maiden in 2:4f., announces that she is faint with love and asks to be sustained with raisins and apples, she is calling for concrete food, to be sure, but *at the same time*, by her choice of fruits that are symbolic of love, she is indicating that only the satisfaction of her desires will bring satisfaction.[2]

While cultural differences and the passage of almost three thousand years make it difficult for us to understand all the implications of these metaphors and symbols, the literal interpretation of the Song requires that the interpreter recognize the connotative associations of these figures and attempt to understand them as clearly as possible.

There is no question that the Song is erotic and sensual. There can be no question that the Song describes sexual encounters between the lovers. At the same time, it must be emphasized that the Song does this in subtle and delicate ways, rather than in the crass and overt ways that many modern commentators suggest. The description of the wedding night in 4:1–5:1 describes the consummation of their marriage in a beautiful and delicate way. No one questions what happened between the lovers, but there is no explicit description of their encounter, such as is found in much love poetry, both ancient and modern.

The focus of the Song is love, not sex. The sexual is recognized as one of the ways love expresses itself in marriage; but it is only one of the ways. The delight of the lovers in one another goes far beyond the explicitly sexual. They enjoy being

---

[2]Gordis, *Song of Songs*, p. 38.

together; they delight in the sound of the other's voice; they find every aspect of the other beautiful and highly desirable. The hair, the nose, the palate, the hands, the fingers, the neck are all charged with excitement because each is a part of the person they love. To look for some explicitly sexual meaning, even if it is said to be hidden or veiled, in every incident and description in the Song is to miss the breadth and comprehensiveness of the love relationship described there.

There is ambiguity in the Song, and many of the statements have a double meaning. This is one of the delightful things about the language of love. Sometimes, the double meaning is part of the playfulness of the lovers as they enjoy one another; sometimes, it contributes to the literary effect by producing an intentional ambiguity. The reader is not sure how to understand the figure. He cannot tell whether the reference was meant to be sexual or not; he cannot be sure "how far to go" in interpreting the figure, just as one lover cannot always be sure exactly what the other has in mind when he or she calls.

For Further Study

1. Read Song of Songs, chapter 1 and try to identify the kinds of parallelism in each verse.

2. Read Song of Songs 4:1–6. Try to determine the common point of comparison in each metaphor and the emphasis of each metaphor used to describe the beloved.

Part 2

Commentary

Outline of Song of Songs

Title (1:1)

I. The Joys and Struggles of Courtship (1:2–3:5)
   A. The Joys and Struggles of Courtship—Part 1 (1:2–2:7)
      1. The Beloved's Desire (1:2–4)
      2. The Beloved's Insecurity (1:5–8)
      3. The Lover's Encouragement (1:9–11)
      4. The Beloved's Thoughts About Her Lover (1:12–14)
      5. The Couple's Dialogue (1:15–2:3)
      6. The Beloved's Desire (2:4–7)
   B. The Courtship Continues—Part 2 (2:8–3:5)
      1. Delight in Her Lover's Arrival (2:8–9)
      2. The Lover's Invitation (2:10–13)
      3. Invitation and Response (2:14–17)
      4. The Beloved's Search for Her Lost Lover (3:1–5)

II. Marriage and Consummation (3:6–5:1)
   A. The Royal Wedding Procession (3:6–11)
   B. The Wedding Night (4:1–5:1)
      1. The Lover's Praise for His Bride (4:1–15)
         a. Praise (4:1–7)
         b. Delight and Desire (4:8–15)
      2. The Beloved's Invitation (4:16)
      3. Consummation (5:1)

Chapter 6

The Joys and Struggles of Courtship
(1:1–2:7)

Title (1:1)

The expression "Song of Songs" is the translation of a Hebrew idiom that usually expresses a superlative idea. The same construction is used in Exodus 26:33 where a distinction is made between the Holy Place in the tabernacle and the Holy of Holies (the Most Holy Place, NIV). Thus, the title of the book means something like "the greatest or best of songs," and perhaps this is to be understood in comparison to the other songs Solomon wrote or as a figurative expression that relates to the subject matter of the book. The title also seems to suggest the unity of the book. The last part of the title, as was noted in the previous discussion of authorship, most likely identifies Solomon as the author of the Song though the Hebrew preposition used here can mean a number of other things besides an indication of the book's authorship. It is of interest to note that many commentators who reject Solomonic authorship of the book still conclude that this is what is intended by the title. Pope, for example, says, "It is, nevertheless, most likely that the intent of the superscription was to attribute the authorship to Solomon."[1]

A. The Joys and Struggles of Courtship—Part 1 (1:2–2:7)

1. The Beloved's Desire (1:2–4)

The Song begins with the girl (the beloved) expressing her desire to be together with her lover and enjoy his caresses and

---

[1] Pope, AB, p. 296.

59

embrace. The Hebrew word translated "love" in verse 2 is used elsewhere in contexts that clearly refer to lovemaking (e.g., Prov. 7:18; Ezek. 16:8 and 23:17) though the parallelism with the first line of the verse suggests that it probably means "caresses" here. She compares the ecstatic effect of his love to that of wine and she finds his love to be far superior.

The mention of perfume or oil (ASV) in verse 3 refers to olive oil in which aromatic spices were blended. This was used for both medicinal and cosmetic purposes, and the aroma produced by this pleased and excited her. While there are difficulties associated with the exact meaning of the words and syntax of verse 3b, "your name is like perfume poured out," she seems to be saying that his name is as pleasing to her as fragrant and expensive perfume. Since in Hebrew culture a person's name was thought synonymous with his character, she may be saying that the character of the king is as pleasing to her as the aroma of perfume. The girl realizes that she is not the only one who recognizes that the person she loves is a wonderful and desirable man, and she admits that they are well justified in their opinion.

In verse 4 the beloved expresses her desire for the king to take her away to his chambers. We have noted above that the decisions that are made about certain introductory matters will again and again have to be applied to the text in interpreting sections that would otherwise be ambiguous, and this must be done here. Both the reference to "love" in verse 2 and the desire for the king to take her to his chambers in verse 4 suggest the possibility of sexual relations. As we have noted earlier, the poetic vignettes that make up the book appear to be arranged in a general order that follows the story of the couple's courtship to their marriage in 3:7–11 with the consummation of the marriage occurring in 4:1–5:1. We have also suggested that the story's canonical context presupposes the moral values of God's covenant with Israel and thus seems to preclude the possibility that a sexual relationship was established prior to the marriage.

Some have suggested that the girl's statement in verse 4 "the king has brought me into his chambers" refers to his "bringing her to the palace chambers where they might see each other more often."[2] Others have suggested that these pictures, while generally arranged in a pattern moving from courtship through marriage to maturity, are not strictly chronological and that the lovers are looking back to their first encounter as a newly married couple. We would suggest that the girl in expressing her desire for her lover is looking forward in anticipation to the time when they would be married and could experience the full physical expression of their love.

Changes in person that would be unacceptable in English prose or poetry are common in Hebrew (and other Semitic languages as well). The girl begins speaking using the third person ("let him kiss me") and then she shifts to the second person ("your love"). The change in the middle of verse 4 to the first person plural ("we rejoice . . . we will praise"), however, appears to indicate a change of speaker. It is likely that these words are spoken by a group of people, and the most plausible identification seems to be the daughters of Jerusalem to whom the girl addresses some of her remarks beginning in verse 5. The daughters of Jerusalem appear throughout the book and may be ladies of the court or those who attend them or simply represent the citizens of Jerusalem in contrast to the girl from the country. They function almost like a chorus throughout the book, sometimes advising the girl or asking her questions, sometimes expressing their praise for what is happening in the relationship between the lovers. Here they praise both the beloved and the lover when they say, "We rejoice and delight in you" (The Hebrew suffix shows that this is directed to the girl.); we will praise your love (the Hebrew suffix shows that this is directed to the lover).

The final sentence of verse 4 seems to come from the beloved, and again it is only the verb form (they love) and the suffix (you, referring to the lover), along with the context, that allows us to identify the various speakers in these verses. Here the beloved is affirming that the affection of these women for her lover is perfectly justified. She seems to be quite secure in her awareness that it is she that her lover cares for and she is not threatened by the obvious affection of these women.

---

[2]Glickman, *Song*, pp. 29–30.

There is a certain mutuality that is evident in these verses and that will be repeated again and again throughout the Song. The girl expresses her affection for her lover and her desire for him. In other instances she seems to clearly initiate their lovemaking. Both the man and the woman are active participants (and initiators) in their relationship. It is interesting to note how the changing cultural perspective has opened up an awareness of this that earlier commentators would not accept. Ginsburg notes that this "aggressiveness" of the woman was taken by some as proof that the Song is an allegory since this is contrary to the nature of women. He notes the argument of Dr. Bennett who took "her solicitous seeking after him" and "her praises of his person" as proof that this is not a human love song. He argued that this is not a matter of cultural differences between the Near East and the West. He said, "It would be more abhorrent from the secluded, submissive character of Eastern brides to ask the gentleman to come and kiss them, than it would be from the dignified confidence of British women. It is not a question of climate or of age, but of *nature*.[3]

2. The Beloved's Insecurity (1:5–8)

While there are several details that are not clear in this section, the basic point of the verses does not appear to be in doubt. The girl's comments in verses 5 and 6 are directed to the daughters of Jerusalem, and seem to imply a prior criticism about the appearance of this girl from the country by these cultured and proper women. She concedes their point about the appearance of her skin, and she explains that this has resulted from her exposure to the sun. Her brothers forced her to take care of the vineyards, perhaps owned by the family, and her work out of doors affected the way she looks.

In verse 5 she says that her brothers made her take care of the vineyards while at the same time she neglected her own vineyard. The reference to her own vineyard is a reference to

---

[3] Dr. Bennett, *Congregational Magazine*, 1838, pp. 148–49, cited by Ginsburg, *Song of Songs*, p. 105. Bennett goes on to say, "Till fishes mount to sing with larks on the shady boughs, and nightengales dive to ocean depths to court the whales, no man, of any age, of any clime, of any rank, can be supposed to write ordinary love songs in such a style."

her body and its appearance. This is a metaphor that is used elsewhere in the Song (8:12 and perhaps 2:15 as well) and along with the metaphor of the garden sometimes has sexual connotations. A vineyard produces wine and the delight and excitement produced by love is compared with that produced by wine throughout the Song (e.g., 1:2, 4). Here the context makes it clear that the figure refers to the girl's physical appearance.

In verse 7 the beloved directs her remarks away from the women who were critical of her and apparently seeks her lover's support and assurance. She describes her lover as a shepherd and expresses her desire to join him where he is tending his sheep. Those who advocate the Shepherd Hypothesis find support for their view as they point out that here the girl clearly describes the one she loves as a shepherd, and they argue that this designation would not be appropriate for Solomon.

The meaning of her description is not entirely clear. It is possible that this description is simply an endearing term that the girl uses for her lover. Some have pointed out that "shepherd" was a conventional term for lovers in the ancient Near East;[4] others have noted that kings in the ancient Near East were frequently referred to as shepherds and thus the term is entirely appropriate as a designation for Solomon. Her choice of this figure to describe Solomon here is perhaps to be explained by the fact that he as the king is the shepherd of his people; at the same time she views her lover as the one she needs to care for her, to protect her and provide for her needs, including her immediate need for encouragement and support in the light of the criticism of the daughters of Jerusalem. She wants to be able to go to her lover while he is away doing his work, and she does not want to be taken for a prostitute (probably the meaning of "veiled woman") as she wanders about looking for him.

The speaker of verse 8 is not certain. Since the girl has just directed her remarks to her lover, it would be expected that he would immediately reply to her remarks, and verse 8 can be understood in that way.[5] It is also possible that these words come from the shepherds who are the "friends" of her lover. It is

---

[4] See the references in Deere, "Meaning," p. 67–68.
[5] This is the way the NIV and NASB translators have understood it.

perhaps best to understand these words as a somewhat sarcastic reply from the daughters of Jerusalem (The daughters of Jerusalem also refer to the beloved as "the most beautiful of women" in 5:9 and 6:1.) to the effect that if she does not know where to find him, then maybe she would be better off going back to the country where she really belongs.

3. The Lover's Encouragement (1:9–11)

The uncertainty and insecurity produced in the beloved by the critical words of the women are relieved by the words of the lover in these verses. He refers to her as "my darling," a term he uses of her nine times throughout the book. Pope has pointed out that mares were not used to pull war chariots in Egypt and has suggested that the lover is saying that this beautiful girl has the same effect on the men as would a mare loose among the stallions of Pharaoh.[6] Thus he is telling his beloved that while the women may not appreciate her beauty and appeal, the men are greatly attracted to her. Fox argues that the chariot mentioned is not necessarily a war chariot and maintains that the point of the comparison is specified in the text as the girl's ornamented beauty.[7] The lover then moves to more specific praise for the beauty of her face and neck adorned and enhanced by the jewelry that she is wearing—perhaps jewelry that would not have measured up to the exacting standards of the sophisticated ladies of Jerusalem. His words must have reassured the beloved, and it appears also to have changed the response, if not the attitude, of the women.

The identity of the speaker in verse 11 is not totally clear, but it appears best to again attribute these words to the daughters of Jerusalem primarily because of the plural "we" indicated by the Hebrew verb form. It is always interesting to see how even the most vigorous and caustic critics often change their opinion, at least overtly, when they hear the opinion of their leader, and that seems to be exactly what is happening

---

[6] Pope, AB, pp. 338–40. Pope cites Egyptian texts describing how those fighting the Egyptian chariot forces would sometimes release a mare in heat to attract the attention of the stallions pulling the chariots and thereby throw the Egyptian army into confusion.

[7] Michael V. Fox, *The Song of Songs and the Ancient Egyptian Love Songs* (Madison, Wisconsin: The University of Wisconsin Press, 1985), p. 105.

here. The response of the king, praising the girl's beauty and affirming his affection for her, brings an immediate change in the women's response as they now volunteer to make fine jewelry for the king's beloved. The lover's praise for his beloved not only reassures and encourages her in the face of criticism from others; it also elevates her reputation in the eyes of those who had been critical of her.

4. The Beloved's Thoughts about Her Lover (1:12–14)

As the girl smelled the fragrance of the nard she was wearing as a perfume,[8] she was reminded of her lover. Nard was an aromatic oil that came from India and was used to make perfume. It was expensive and thus was perhaps a gift from Solomon. The fragrant odor of the nard became for her a figure of her lover. She compares him to a pouch of myrrh, another expensive aromatic resin from Arabia and northern Africa, that passes the night between her breasts. He is in her thoughts as pervasive and as delightful as a sweet smelling perfume.

Finally, she compares him to "a cluster of henna blossoms from the vineyards of En Gedi." En Gedi is a beautiful and fertile oasis in the barren desert along the western side of the Dead Sea, and she describes her lover as a beautiful and delicate flower in the midst of this fertile oasis. While the primary use of henna was to make a dye used in cosmetics and for dyeing clothes, there is also evidence that it was used to make perfume,[9] and all the figures used here have that element in common.

5. The Couple's Dialogue (1:15–2:3)

This section captures the couple in their praise of one another, perhaps at a time when they are alone. In view of the figures used in verses 16–17, some have suggested that the couple are alone during a walk in the forest. It is difficult to

---

[8]The meaning of the first part of verse 12 is not entirely clear. The Hebrew word translated "table" in NIV and NASB is uncertain. It does mean "table" in later Hebrew; in the other three instances where it is used in the Old Testament, it means either "surrounding area" or "round about." It seems likely that the girl sees the king at a distance and this combined with the fragrance of her perfume triggers these thoughts.

[9]Deere, "Meaning," p. 79 and the references in n. 2.

decide where this section ends because the girl's remarks beginning in 2:3 continue through 2:13, and it seems strange to divide the section in the middle of her speech. At the same time, her remarks in 2:3 are obviously a direct response to the king's words in 2:2, and so we have chosen to divide the section between verses 2 and 3 despite the fact that this interrupts her speech.

The couple's mutual praise in these verses involves each partner repeating expressions used by the other and then expanding on what the other has said. The king begins by emphasizing to his beloved that she is beautiful, and then he adds that her eyes are doves. The exact meaning of this is unclear. Some interpreters have suggested that he means that her eyes are like a dove's eyes; others have suggested that he is talking about the shape of her eyes or the glistening color of her eyes. Some have suggested that it is the courtship behavior of doves that stands behind this figure and that her eyes reveal her love for him; others have suggested that it is the nature of a dove that is in view here and that her eyes (or countenance) reflect her peaceful and gentle character.

The beloved replies using a masculine form of the same word that her lover used for her ("beautiful" in v. 15 and "handsome" in v. 16), and she adds that he is pleasant ("charming," NIV). As Deere points out, the Hebrew conjunction used here introduces something unexpected and suggests that the word "pleasant" or "charming" is not strictly parallel to the word "beautiful."[10] Her comment may then apply to his personality rather than just to his appearance.

The girl then describes what is most likely their resting place in the forest, under the trees as their bed and house (The Hebrew uses the plural "our houses"). The Hebrew word translated "bed" is a general one and there are a number of things that two lovers could do on their bed under the trees. The text makes no explicit reference to their activities and the decision that is made in this regard will depend on the prior judgments made by the interpreter concerning the development of the story and the purpose of the book. Some see this as a part

---

[10] Ibid., pp. 83–84.

of the fertility cult; others see this as a sexual encounter between the two unmarried lovers; still others see this as a statement made in anticipation of a sexual relationship after marriage. It seems to the present author that the girl's words need reflect nothing more than the fact that they were enjoying one another's company and love in a place where the beauty of nature around simply enhanced their enjoyment of their time together. Certainly, there have been many young lovers who walked together in the words, stopped under the trees, and enjoyed one another's company and caresses without a sexual encounter. Her words here neither require the conclusion that they had sexual intercourse, nor preclude that possibility, and a decision about that will depend on the interpreter's judgment.

The girl compares herself to a flower in 2:1, and while the exact identification of the plants that she mentions is uncertain, the first, which NIV translates "rose of Sharon," is probably a member of the crocus family that grew in Sharon, the coastal plain in northern Israel. The second flower mentioned is some kind of lily, though not the flower that we call Lily of the Valley. There is difference of opinion as to what she means by this comparison. Some think that modesty requires that she not be praising herself, and they understand her to be saying, in effect, "I am nothing but one of the wild flowers that grow abundantly and cover the valley." Others suggest that she is praising herself, and they conclude that it is the praise and encouragement of her lover that has made the difference between her apology in 1:5–6 and this positive comparison of herself to a beautiful flower.[11] The verse would then affirm the power of love and praise to transform a person's opinion of himself or herself—a power that many people fail to utilize in their dealings with those they love.

The lover then takes the figure the girl has used to describe herself and changes it into even greater praise of her beauty. She has said that she is the lily of the valleys; he now says that

---

[11] Both Glickman (*Song*, p. 39) and Deere ("Meaning," p. 86) make this point and as Deere points out the Hebrew construction seems to favor the conclusion that it is a specific flower (the rose, the lily) to which she compares herself. Deere says, "She came to believe that she was beautiful and significant because she was so in his eyes."

she is like a lily among the thorns in comparison to the other maidens (So NIV; the Hebrew word is "daughters," perhaps a specific reference to the daughters of Jerusalem who criticized her before.). Thus, in his eyes her beauty stands out above that of the other women as a single beautiful lily would stand out in a field of thorn bushes.

The beloved responds to her lover's compliment by saying that in comparison to other men, he is like an apple (or perhaps an apricot) tree[12] in a forest of other trees. She delights to sit in his shade, and this is symbolic of protection since shade provides needed relief from the heat of the sun. She enjoys the fruit that he produces, and this is probably symbolic of the provision and sustenance that he gives her.

6. The Beloved's Desire (2:4–7)

In the present author's opinion, the best understanding of these verses finds their setting in a banquet hall, though the Hebrew expression "the house of wine" can be understood in almost as many ways as the literal rendering suggests in English. The king's love for his beloved was obvious for all to see, and this clearly identified her as belonging to him, just as the banners (NIV "standard") of the various tribes in Numbers publicly identified the troops belonging to those tribes (e.g., Num. 2:3, 10).

The king's obvious affection for the girl aroused in her a deep desire to express physically her love for him, and she complains that she is sick because she is unable to express that love. As White points out, the theme of lovesickness is often found in Egyptian love poetry. In one example cited by him, a young man complains about this sickness and says about his girlfriend, "She will make the doctors unnecessary because she knows my sickness."[13] The beloved suggests a remedy for her faintness and the foods she asks for, raisin cakes and apples, are foods that are symbolic of love. As Gordis suggests, "she is

---

[12] Deere ("Meaning," p. 87, n. 2) summarizes the evidence and concludes that it is probably the cultivated apple tree that is referred to here. The identification of this fruit remains uncertain.

[13] John B. White, *A Study of the Language of Love in the Song of Songs and Ancient Egyptian Poetry*, SBL Dissertation Series 38 (Missoula, Montana: Scholar's Press, 1978), p. 105.

calling for concrete food, to be sure, but *at the same time,* by her choice of fruits that are symbolic of love, she is indicating that only the satisfaction of her desires will bring her healing."[14] Her words in verse 6 make it clear that her desire is to have her lovesickness cured through having her lover make love to her.

Verse 7 constitutes a refrain that occurs two other times in the book (3:5 and 8:4), and in all three instances the words seem to come at the end of major sections of the book. It seems likely that the words are spoken by the girl, and it is clear that the daughters of Jerusalem are called on to take a solemn oath, whose exact significance is not clear. Those who assume that the previous verses describe a sexual encounter between the couple understand the verses to mean that the couple is not to be disturbed until they have finished their lovemaking, though the verb used here normally means "to arouse to activity" or "to awake" rather than "to disturb." Those who advocate the Shepherd Hypothesis suppose that the daughters are being admonished not to try to encourage her to transfer her affection away from her shepherd lover about whom she has been thinking to Solomon. Glickman suggests that the girl, despite her very strong desire for the physical consummation of their relationship, realizes that this must wait until after they are married. He understands her words as a call for patience, both to the other women and to herself, until it is appropriate to express love fully in marriage.[15]

In view of the way this refrain is used elsewhere in the book, it seems likely that the primary purpose of the refrain is to emphasize that the kind of relationship described in the book cannot be forced. It must develop and express itself in the proper way and at the proper time. Here, as Deere suggests, the refrain is a warning to the daughters of Jerusalem, who are excited by this example of the delight and passion of love that they are seeing between the beloved and her lover and who are desirous of the same experience. She advises them "not to force love but to wait for it patiently so that it might come to them at the right time."[16] The refrain also stands as a warning to the

---

[14] Gordis, *Song,* p. 38.
[15] Glickman, *Song,* p. 44.
[16] Deere, "Meaning," p. 97.

beloved not to allow her desire for physical intimacy to express itself at this point in their relationship; it is a warning to the daughters of Jerusalem not to encourage this expression of love prematurely. The refrain affirms that the physical expression of love must not be forced or rushed until it can be properly expressed in the context of marriage.

This conclusion about the significance of the refrain is appropriate in the context, and it is consistent with the point made in 8:7, which most agree is the climax of the book. Implicit in this is the idea that the physical and the erotic aspect of love is properly the result of love rather than the means to it. This is certainly a point that Solomon would have understood very well.

For Further Study

1. Read Exod. 20:14; Lev. 18:20, 20:10; Deut. 5:18, 22:13–29; Prov. 2:16–19, 5:1–23, 6:23–35, 7:6–27; 1 Cor. 6:15–18; Heb. 13:4. What do these passages suggest about the question of whether the sexual experience of the lovers takes place outside the context of marriage?

2. What role does the lover's praise and encouragement of his beloved play in this section? How does it affect the way she feels about herself; how does it affect the way other people feel about her? How do you think his praise for her affects their relationship?

Chapter 7

The Courtship Continues

(2:8–3:5)

B. The Courtship Continues—Part 2 (2:8–3:5)

1. Delight in Her Lover's Arrival (2:8–9)

These verses begin a beautiful poem about the delight and excitement of the two lovers as they are together in the country in the spring. Verse 8 captures the excitement of the girl as her lover approaches, and her description of his approach is filled with the kind of hyperbole that is typical of lovers and which vividly communicates something of the intensity of her feelings. Her description of him as a gazelle and a stag refers to his swiftness, his beauty, and his grace as well as to his virility. It is clear that the excitement over their meeting is mutual in that he is anxious to catch a glimpse of his beloved through the window.

2. The Lover's Invitation (2:10–13)

In these verses the lover's invitation to come outside in order to enjoy the delights of spring are reported by the girl, and this initial section of his words to her begin and end with the words, "Arise, my darling, my beautiful one, and come with me" (vv. 10 and 13). As many have pointed out, the special connection between love and springtime is found throughout the world's literature. This seems to be the case because when two people are in love there is a beauty and freshness to life that was not the case before. Glickman says, "Whenever any couple falls in love, it is spring for them because their lives are fresh; everything in life has a new perspective; what was black and white is now in color; what was dark is light."[1] In verse 12, a Hebrew word is used that can be translated either "pruning" (as in NASB) or "singing" (as in NIV), and it is difficult to decide which is the better translation. The translation "pruning" is easier to defend linguistically, but pruning normally is done when the plants are dormant rather than in the spring. Although a unique connection between the singing of birds and spring is not readily apparent, many prefer to see this as a reference to the singing of birds, especially since the cooing of doves is mentioned in the next line.

3. Invitation and Response (2:14–17)

The lover in verse 14 refers to his beloved as "my dove in the clefts of the rock." The preceeding verses suggest that she was still inside the house and that his invitation was coming through the latticework and windows. Thus he describes her as a little bird that makes its nest in inaccessible and hidden places on the mountainside. He wants her to come out to him where they can be alone together and where he can enjoy hearing her voice and looking at her. The Hebrew word translated "face" in the NIV means "appearance" and the word here refers to her overall form or appearance rather than just to her face.

A number of difficulties are associated with the interpretation of verse 15. It is uncertain who the speaker is, though it seems best to assign these words to the girl. The one to whom the words are directed is not entirely clear because the word "catch" is masculine plural. It seems probable that the girl is quoting a proverb and that she is directing it to her lover and requesting that he overcome the problems that could potentially ruin their relationship (this is almost certainly what the vineyard represents here) and prevent it from getting past the bloom stage and developing into the ripe fruit of marriage.[2]

As is often the case in this kind of literature and this kind of dialogue between lovers, there is a certain ambiguity that probably even the lovers cannot and need not resolve. Certainly the context suggests that an immediate obstacle that had to be

---

[1] Glickman, Song, pp. 46–47.

[2] As Deere ("Meaning," pp. 102–103) points out, "The destructive tendencies of foxes in regard to vineyards were proverbial in the ancient world."

resolved was getting her out of the house so they could be alone together. In the Egyptian love poetry—and in the common experience of mankind—a problem that lovers often encounter is the resistance of parents and family and their attempts to keep the lovers apart. It is possible that 8:8–9 speaks of the efforts of the girl's brothers to protect her, and thus what they viewed as necessary and appropriate protection may well have been viewed by the girl and her lover as a significant obstacle to their relationship developing as it should.

Certainly the problems that could keep the relationship from developing into what it could become are many and varied, and the application of the principle suggested here is as broad as the parameters of human experience in male-female relationships. The point that is made here is a crucial one, however. This couple understood that problems have the potential for destroying their relationship and they were determined to address the problems and solve them. Their commitment to the relationship generated a firm resolve to creatively deal with the problems so that their relationship could progress.

Their commitment to the relationship is expressed by the beloved in verse 16 when she says, "My lover is mine and I am his," an affirmation that is repeated in a slightly modified form in 6:3 and 7:10. The meaning of her statement at the end of verse 16, "he browses among the lilies," is obscure, but perhaps the figure is related to her earlier description of him as a gazelle (2:9), which she will repeat in the next verse. W. M. Thompson noted in the last century that "gazelles still delight to feed on them (lilies), and you can scarcely ride through the woods north of Tabor, where the lilies abound, without frightening them from their flowery pastures."[3] At the same time it seems likely that "browsing among the lilies" is a metaphor for his enjoyment of his beloved's charms; this is also the case in 6:2–3.

There are several difficulties in interpreting verse 17. It is unclear whether the Hebrew expression "when the day blows" refers to the evening when the cool breezes blow (as NASB) or to the morning (as NIV) which is perhaps more consistent with the shadows fleeing in the second line of the verse. It is unclear

---

[3]W. M. Thompson, *The Land and the Book*, p. 256, cited by Deere, "Meaning," p. 105, n. 3.

whether the girl is instructing her lover to turn in order to leave her or whether she is asking him to return to her since the Hebrew can be understood either way. Finally the meaning of the expression translated "rugged hills" by NIV is quite uncertain. One plausible suggestion is to see it as a place name, "mountains of Bether," in which case she is instructing him to leave like a stag or gazelle bounding over the mountains, just as he came at the beginning of the section (2:8–9).

The Hebrew word *bathar* means "to divide" and there is a noun *bether* that refers to a piece of meat that has been cut in two as part of the ritual associated with making a covenant (Gen. 15:10 and Jer. 34:18). The first part of this verse is repeated in 4:6, in a description of the couple's lovemaking on their wedding night, and it is possible that the "mountains of Bether" is "her very delicate and restrained reference to her breasts."[4] Thus she would be expressing her desire for physical intimacy, a desire that cannot be realized until they are married. If this suggestion is correct, the lover's words in 4:6 would be a reference back to her stated desire for sexual intimacy as those desires are fulfilled on their wedding night.

4. Search for Her Lost Lover (3:1–5)

This section is taken by most commentators as a description of a dream that the girl had, and support for this is found in the similarities between this section and the dream reported in 5:2–8. The dream was prompted by her fear of losing her lover, perhaps as their relationship had developed to the point where marriage was contemplated or even agreed to. The intensity of both the girl's love and her fears is emphasized by the repetition of words like "seek," "could not find," and "the one my heart loves." She is expressing what seems to be a universal fear of losing something very, very important to a person; the imagination dwells on this possibility, and the imagination seems more vivid and the possibility even more real at night. In this instance, whether in reality or in her dream, the girl gets up and begins to search diligently for her lover. Finally, when she finds

---

[4]Glickman, *Song*, p. 17.

him, she embraces him and clings to him in determination not to let him go until she brings him to her mother's house.

Most commentators assume that her purpose in taking him to her house and into the room where she was conceived—certainly one of the most secure places that the girl would know—was to make love. Deere, however, notes the suggestion of Campbell who says, "the 'mother's house' was the locus for matters pertinent to marriage, especially for discussion and planning for marriage."[5] Deere concludes that her purpose in bringing him to her mother's house was to make final plans for marriage "so that she might never have to lose him again."[6]

Again, there is the exhortation to the daughters of Jerusalem not to force love, and in this can be seen both a symmetry and a development of the plot. As was the case with the same exhortation in 2:7, this refrain emphasizes to the daughters of Jerusalem that this kind of relationship cannot be forced but must be allowed to develop in its own way and at its own pace. The exhortation again comes at a point where the possibility of sexual intimacy has been suggested, and again its purpose is also to encourage patience in expressing their love. It is a call to wait for marriage where the sexual expression of love is appropriate rather than succumb to the temptation that their desire for one another presents. The literary symmetry is also evident because the girl is "rewarded" immediately after the exhortation of 2:7 by the appearance of her lover bounding over the mountains; she is rewarded after the exhortation of 3:5 by the appearance of Solomon coming to Jerusalem for his wedding. This also suggests a development in the plot because their relationship has now progressed through their courtship to the point of marriage. The first major section of the book is concluded, and a transition is provided into the wedding section of the book.

For Further Study

1. Recall the delight and excitement that you felt toward your mate before you were married. What can you do to rekindle some of that excitement?

---

[5] Edward Campbell, *Ruth*, Anchor Bible (Garden City, New York: Doubleday, 1975), p. 64.

[6] Deere, "Meaning," p. 114.

2. What obstacles and problems did you encounter in your courtship that had the potential for preventing your relationship from developing? Are there "little foxes" in your present relationship with your spouse that need to be captured before they do damage to the relationship?

Chapter 8

Marriage and Consummation
(3:6–5:1)

A. The Royal Wedding Procession (3:6–11)

The mention of the day of Solomon's wedding in verse 7 makes it clear that these verses describe a royal wedding procession. The elaborate ceremony and celebration associated with the wedding of a king are described, including the military attendants in full regalia and the costly and ornate carriage/sedan chair that the king had made especially for his wedding. These verses also capture something of the excitement felt by the bride and groom, their family and friends, and in this instance, by the entire country as well.

While the general context of these verses seems to be established by verse 7, there are several details that remain unclear. The answer to the question of verse 6, "Who is this coming up from the desert?" is not clear. An apparent answer to the question is found in verse 7, "Look! It is Solomon's carriage." The Hebrew interrogative pronoun translated "who" seems to require that the answer involve a person rather than a thing. One might conclude that Solomon is the answer to the question because it is his carriage that is described as coming up from the desert, but a problem for that interpretation is created by the fact that the Hebrew pronoun translated "this" is feminine rather than the masculine that would be expected if Solomon were the antecedent of the pronoun and the answer to the question. It is possible that the Hebrew pronoun translated "who" is used here in the meaning "what" (a meaning it occasionally has elsewhere in the Hebrew Bible), in which case the answer to the question could be the carriage of Solomon (perhaps with him in it). The Hebrew word "carriage" is a feminine noun that does agree in gender with the pronoun "this." This is perhaps the most likely solution though it must be pointed out that the same question, "who is this?" occurs again in 8:5, where it refers to the girl leaning on her lover.

There is also uncertainty about the exact nature of the carriage/couch in verse 7 and the carriage/litter/sedan chair mentioned in verse 9, although it is possible that the two Hebrew words refer to the same thing, as is suggested by the NIV translation of the different Hebrew words as "carriage" in verses 7 and 9. The word used in verse 7 normally means "couch" or "bed." The word used in verse 9 occurs only here in the Hebrew Bible and is generally understood as referring to the litter or sedan chair, in which people of high rank were carried in the ancient world.

There is also uncertainty as to the purpose for which the carriage described here was used. Some have suggested that it was made to transport Solomon in procession to his wedding. Others, based on the feminine pronoun used in the question of verse 6 as well as on the fact that the word used in verse 9 is used in later Hebrew to refer to the litter on which a bride was carried, have concluded that this is a description of the carriage that Solomon had made to carry his bride in the wedding procession. The text is ambiguous, but the literary symmetry noted above in the discussion of the refrain in 3:5 suggests that these verses most likely describe Solomon's coming to Jerusalem for his wedding.

B. The Wedding Night (4:1–5:1)

1. The Lover's Praise for His Bride (4:1–15)

This section, containing the lover's praise for his bride, can be divided into two distinct sections. Verses 1–7 begin and end with "How beautiful you are, my darling," and contain descriptive praise for various physical features of his beloved. Verses 9–15 describe the effect her beauty has on him and the anticipation of their physical intimacy for the first time. The context of these verses, immediately following the wedding procession of 3:6-11 and just before the sexual consummation of their relationship described in 5:1, clearly suggests that they describe the couple's wedding night. This is further indicated by the mention of her veil in 4:1, since the evidence suggests that women did wear veils on their wedding day but did not normally wear them either before or after that time.[1] See also the comments on 1:7.

The king praises the physical features of his bride in a general sequence beginning at her head and descending to her breasts, and he does this using a number of metaphors whose exact point is not always clear. As was noted in the introduction, these figures of speech are meant to communicate to the beloved and to the reader how the king feels as he delights in the physical beauty of his bride at this special moment in their relationship.

The king begins his praise of his bride's beauty using the same words that he used earlier in 1:15 ("your eyes are doves"), but he here adds the words "behind your veil." It has already been suggested that the reference to her veil suggests that this scene took place on their wedding night. Fox suggests that the reference to her eyes as "doves behind your veil" suggests not only the delicacy and softness of her eyes but other characteristics of the dove as well. He says, "The dove is bashful and hides in inaccessible places. So too the eyes of the Shulammite hide behind her veil, a quality that adds to their fascination. . . . Her eyes are like doves calling to the youth from their hiding place. They arouse in him longing and desire to reach her."[2]

Next the king says that her "hair is like a flock of goats descending from Mount Gilead." It seems likely that this metaphor has a visual dimension; goats in Palestine are usually black or dark brown, as, no doubt, was the color of his beloved's hair. The figure of the goats descending down a distant hillside suggests the dark glistening hair gently flowing over her

---

[1] In Gen. 24:65 Rebekah covered herself with a veil when she realized that the man she was approaching was her future husband, and verse 67 suggests that their marriage took place almost immediately after the servant presented his report of what happened to Isaac. It was presumably the veil that Leah was wearing that contributed to Jacob's failure to recognize her until after their marriage had been consummated (Gen. 29:21–25). For a summary of the evidence see Deere, "Meaning," pp. 136–39.

[2] Fox, *Song of Songs*, p. 129.

shoulders and down her back. It is further possible that this image recalled similar scenes that the two had enjoyed together and that the force of his metaphor was intensified by those shared experiences in the country.

In verse two the lover praises the beautiful teeth of his beloved by comparing them with sheared and washed ewes. The point of the comparison seems to involve both the whiteness and the evenness of the girl's teeth. The ewes are described as "each having its twin" (NIV) or as "all of which bear twins" (NASB). The Hebrew verb form seems to favor the NASB translation here; the NIV reflects the fact that it is the completeness and symmetry of the teeth that is being emphasized. In addition, the bearing of twins seems to have been rare and thus the statement that "all" bear twins would be hyperbole in the extreme. Pope has suggested that multiple births were so rare as to be regarded as a special manifestation of divine favor. He goes on to add that "If twinning among sheep was rare, perfectly matched teeth may also have been unusual and thus all the more appreciated."[3] The figure describes beautiful and perfectly matched teeth without any gaps or flaws.

Verse 3 describes her lips/mouth, and the poetic parallelism suggests that no distinction is made between lips and mouth here. One point of emphasis is obviously the red color of her lips, perhaps the result of using some kind of cosmetic. Whether there is significance in the mention of a thread is not clear, but it may emphasize the delicate outline of her mouth.

The comparison of the beloved's temples with a slice of pomegranate has proved difficult for commentators to understand. As Ginsburg has pointed out, the comparison between a girl's cheeks and the pomegranate is found several times in Near Eastern love poetry.[4] Since the Hebrew word translated "temples" is used only here and in Judges 4–5, the story of Jael killing Sisera by driving a tent peg through his temple while he slept, it has been suggested that the word actually refers to the side of the face and thus describes the girl's cheeks rather than her temples. The point of the comparison with a pomegranate is not clear, and numerous suggestions have been made regarding

[3] Pope, *AB*, p. 462.
[4] Ginsburg, *Song of Songs*, p. 158.

this. The most obvious possibility, if the reference is to the girl's cheeks rather than her temples, would be a comparison of the red color of the pomegranate skin with the color of her cheeks. However, if this is the point of the comparison, it is not clear why her temple or cheek is compared to a slice of pomegranate. Marcia Falk has suggested that in a slice of pomegranate there are red seeds seen through a white membrane, and she concludes, "Might this not be like ruddy skin glimpsed through a mesh of white veil?"[5]

If the reference is to the girl's temples, it is hard to see why this would be a point of beauty singled out for praise. Deere has suggested that the point of the comparison may be that even such a feature as his new bride's temple is something fascinating and beautiful to the groom on this special occasion. He further notes that the pomegranate was known both for its color and for its sweetness. He suggests that "the idea of sweetness hints at the Lover's desire to kiss the temples and cheeks of the Beloved."[6] The mention of pomegranate wine in Egyptian love poetry and its use in love potions may add intensity to the comparison as well.

The meaning of the description of the bride's neck in verse 4 is difficult because of several words in the verse whose exact meaning is not certain. The "tower of David" is mentioned only here in the Hebrew Bible; the word translated "elegant" in NIV (which seems like an unlikely translation of the word) and "with rows of stones" in NASB occurs only here, and there is no consensus among scholars as to what the word means, as is evident from the very different renderings found among the various English translations. The general picture presented in the metaphor is clear; it describes a tower on the wall of a city that is decorated with soldier's shields and perhaps other weapons as well. This may be similar to the situation described in Ezekiel 27:10–11, where mercenary soldiers from various places who served in the army of Tyre hung their shields and helmets on the wall of the city "bringing you splendor" (v. 10). According to verse 11, "They hung their shields around your

[5] Marcia Falk, *Love Lyrics From the Bible* (Sheffield: The Almond Press, 1982), p. 84.

[6] Deere, "Meaning," p. 141.

walls; they brought your beauty to perfection." It is possible, given the evidence of this text and other ancient texts describing the use of shields as building decorations, that the tower was actually decorated with shields and weapons, though some have suggested that the masonry with its courses of stones simply had the appearance of being decorated with shields.

Pope has pointed out that necklaces consisting of multiple layers that resemble masonry layers of brick or stone are known from various parts of the ancient world[7] and it is possible that this is what the king is describing in these verses. It is true that in every other instance the beloved's praise for his bride has centered on parts of her body rather than jewelry or the like. Even so, it seems likely that the king compares his bride, her neck ornamented with beautiful layered necklaces, with the magnificent and impressive tower on the wall of the city. In so doing he is affirming not only the great beauty of his beloved but also the impact that her stately and elegant appearance has on him.

Next her breasts are described as "twin fawns of a gazelle that browse among the lilies." This picture of the fawns peacefully eating among the lilies is a scene of quiet beauty. Describing her breasts as fawns, no doubt, was intended to emphasize that they were soft and delicate. As Deere suggests, "Just as one looks on a fawn and naturally wants to stroke its soft coat, so the Lover desired to caress the breasts of his bride."[8]

In this unit, the king has praised seven features of his bride, a number that often symbolizes perfection in the Bible. Here that significance of the number seven seems to be confirmed in verse 7, where the lover concludes this unit by saying, "All beautiful you are, my darling; there is no flaw in you."

Before the unit ends in verse 7, however, there is a shift from the praise for her beauty that has characterized 4:1–5 to a statement of his desire for her—a desire that, no doubt, has been intensified by his enjoyment of her beauty. His words in verse 6 repeat her earlier words to him in 2:17. As was noted in our discussion of that verse, it is uncertain whether she was expressing her desire for sexual intimacy—a desire that could

---

[7] Pope, AB, pp. 467–68 and 454, fig. 7.
[8] Deere, "Meaning," p. 145.

not be properly realized prior to marriage—or whether she was simply instructing him to leave in the same way that he came. It is clear that he is recalling that experience and is indicating that they can now, in the context of marriage, fulfill that which they had earlier desired. Now he will go to the mountain of myrrh and the hill of incense, and the context clearly suggests that these expressions refer to her breasts. This is also suggested by her earlier comment in 1:13 where she had spoken of a sachet of myrrh between her breasts.

Verses 8–15 continue the lover's praise of his beloved though now in more general terms than in the previous section. The lover also emphasizes the effect she has on him and expresses his desire to enjoy to the full the delights of her love. The fact that the beloved is referred to five times in this section as "bride," while not proving the couple is now married (The word can also refer to a girl who is engaged or it could simply be a term of endearment like "sister."), does constitute strong additional evidence to support that conclusion. Even as the lover expresses his desire for his bride and describes the effect of her beauty and love on him, there appears to be a certain reluctance on the part of the beloved, which prevents her from being a fully willing partner in their lovemaking. Perhaps this was a fear that existed despite her deep desire to experience physical intimacy with her lover; it was, no doubt, the fear that often results from uncertainty over that which has never been experienced. This is suggested by his invitation to "come from Lebanon . . . from the den of lions," etc. The places mentioned by the lover in verse 8 probably have little to do with actual geography but rather represent places that are distant and potentially dangerous. This reluctance on the part of the bride is further suggested by the lover's description of her in verse 12 as "a garden locked up . . . a spring enclosed, a sealed fountain." Despite his enchantment with her and the intoxicating effect her beauty and love have on him, despite his intense desire for her, he wants her as a fully willing partner in their lovemaking, and he waits for her invitation before enjoying the full delights that her love can provide.

The metaphor of the girl as a locked garden, as Fox points out, "both expresses the boy's desire for greater intimacy . . .

and praises the girl's modesty and sexual exclusiveness."[9] The metaphor of a spring is also used in Proverbs 5:15–18 as a figure of a woman's sexuality. The metaphors of the beloved as a garden and a spring suggest refreshment, nourishment, and enjoyment; fruit is produced by a garden, and vital, life-giving water comes forth from a spring. The garden described in 4:13–14 is a tropical delight filled with all kinds of expensive and rare delicacies. As Deere suggests, it is "a total delight to the senses of the Lover, an extravagance of beauty."[10]

2. The Beloved's Invitation to Her Lover (4:16)

In response to her lover's praise and request, the beloved, in beautiful and delicate words, invites her lover to possess her. She continues the figures he has used to describe her and requests that the wind blow and stir up the fragrant spices that he said were growing in her garden so as to make her even more appealing to her lover. Then she invites him to come into her garden, which she now describes as his garden, and taste its choice fruits.

3. The Marriage Consummated (5:1)

This verse indicates that the lover has accepted his bride's invitation and that he has entered the previously locked garden and has enjoyed its delicacies to the full. As Deere points out, "The verbs 'come,' 'gathered,' 'eaten,' and 'drunk' mark a total and satisfying experience of the garden."[11] The fact that the previously locked garden has now become his is evident from the possessive suffix "my" (my garden, my sister, my myrrh, my spice, etc.) that occurs eight times in only sixteen words in this verse.

The experience of their first sexual encounter is described in a beautiful and delicate way. There is little debate about what these verses are describing and yet the experience is related in a way that elevates the experience above the coarse and purely sensual. The beauty of the experience is conveyed through the delicate poetry. Their sexual intercourse in marriage is seen as the proper physical expression of their tender and intense love

---

[9] Fox, Song, p. 137.
[10] Deere, "Meaning," p. 158.
[11] Deere, "Meaning," p. 162.

for each other. Theirs is a "one flesh" relationship that involves a growing emotional, spiritual, and intellectual unity, and their physical oneness is not isolated and independent of that broader oneness. Underlying the message of the Song is the idea that God made man and woman for this kind of relationship. The Song describes the physical aspect of their relationship in a way that affirms that this part of their relationship is a gracious gift of God to mankind. The book also presupposes that the gift will be accepted and enjoyed by man in a way that is consistent with His Law. The way the Song describes the sexual relationship between the lover and his beloved affirms, if only in an implicit way, the beauty of this gift of God as God intended it to be expressed.

The plural forms used in the final line of 5:1 make it clear that these words are not spoken by the lovers but are directed to them by some unnamed third party. The identity of the speaker of the words is debated. Some have suggested that it is the daughters of Jerusalem who speak the words like a chorus; some have suggested that these words come from the guests at the wedding who are continuing to celebrate even as the couple has retired to their private quarters; some have suggested that these words come from the author of the poem and represent his editorial comment at this point; one commentator has suggested that it is God who speaks these words in approval and encouragement for their lovemaking. Despite uncertainty as to the speaker of these words, the significance of the words is clearly to encourage and affirm the lovers in their enjoyment of each other.

For Further Study

1. Despite the excitement and desire of the husband, a restraint is also evident in 4:1–15. What does this suggest about the character of love and the mutuality of the "one flesh" relationship as intended by God?

2. How do marriage relationships typically change from what is described in this honeymoon scene? In what ways are these changes good? In what ways are they bad? What can be done to retain an appropriate degree of this romantic intensity as a marriage matures?

Chapter 9

Moving Toward Maturity, Part 1
(5:2–6:13)

The last major section of the book (5:2–8:4) describes the development of the couple's relationship after their marriage, and there are several parallels between this section and both the courtship and wedding sections of the book. Perhaps this is to indicate that while the relationship is made permanent through their mutual commitment in marriage the basic nature of their relationship does not change. From one perspective, marriage seems to represent the ultimate level in the relationship between a man and a woman; new ways of expressing their love are available to them, and there is a new security that comes from the unconditional commitment of both partners to the relationship that is the basis for marriage as God intended it. From another perspective, marriage simply continues the same relationship at a different level. There are new possibilities for intimacy of spirit and emotion as well as for physical intimacy, but the "one flesh" relationship that begins at marriage only begins at that point. Relationships are dynamic and they continue to change because the people involved in them continue to change.

Sometimes the excitement and romance that characterize almost every newly married couple gives way not to a deepening and more mature love for one another but rather to a complacency in the relationship that takes the other person for granted and fails to appreciate and respond to his or her needs and desires. These verses describe a situation like that along with the unfortunate consequences that resulted and the steps that were taken to resolve the problem. The section also describes the delight and enjoyment of one another that was the continuing experience of the two as they were reconciled and as their relationship deepened and matured.

A. Tension and Reconciliation (5:2–6:13)

1. Unresponsiveness, Separation, and Search (5:2–8)

Most commentators understand this section as something that the girl experienced in a dream, though this does not seem to be a necessary conclusion. What is clear, however, is the experience that it describes and the problem that her unresponsiveness created for their relationship. The lover came to the door of her room and asked his beloved to open the door for him, using several of the terms of endearment that had been used by him in 5:1. The discomfort of the lover is indicated in his description of himself as being drenched with dew so his motive for seeking entry does not seem to have been limited to his desire to make love. The beloved's response to her lover's request was to indicate that since she was already dressed for bed, it would be too much of an inconvenience for her to get up to open the door for him.

Verse 4 indicates that the lover tried to get into the room by reaching through the hole in the door in an attempt to unlatch the door, bolted from the inside, without the key. At this point, her sympathy for her husband (the Hebrew expression translated "my heart began to pound for him" in NIV literally means "my insides murmured [or perhaps gurgled] for him," and it normally means to have feelings of sympathy or compassion.) prompted her to open the door. Unfortunately, her husband had already gone by this time, and she found only myrrh on the door handle as a sign of his presence. It is possible, given the connection of myrrh with sexual activity in Proverbs 7:17–18, that this indicates his desire to make love.

As soon as the beloved saw that her husband was gone, her heart sank, no doubt, because she realized that her delayed response had created a problem that she had not intended to create. She called to her lover, but there was no answer; she sought him out but was unable to find him. She was harrassed by the watchmen in the city and she finally calls on the daughters of Jerusalem to help her find her lost lover.

There are clear parallels between this section and the events related in 2:1–5. Both incidents took place at night while the girl was in bed, and both perhaps took place in a dream or in the girl's thoughts rather than in actuality. Both instances involved her lost lover and her attempt to find him; the watchmen of the city were encountered in each and the daughters of Jerusalem were involved in some way each time. There are differences as well because the girl found her lost lover in chapter 2 but was unable to locate him in this section. The function of the daughters of Jerusalem is different in the two sections, too. In chapter 5, the reason for the separation between the girl and her lover is given, while in the earlier chapter no reason is suggested. Certainly, these literary parallels contribute to the artistic quality of the Song; they may further suggest that there are basic elements in a relationship between a man and a woman that remain constant both before and after marriage.

This section describes a relationship that is encountered in virtually every marriage relationship and can sometimes lead to serious problems in the relationship. In this instance the girl delayed in responding to her lover's overt signals—his pounding at the door and his explicit request to open the door to him—and this caused a separation in their relationship, a situation that she immediately set about to resolve. In most circumstances, however, the signals that are ignored or to which there is a delayed response (perhaps because of preoccupation with other things or a desire not to be inconvenienced or a lack of appreciation for the other person or whatever) are in the beginning, at least, far more subtle than the ones mentioned here. The lack of sensitivity to the needs and desires of the other person almost always has a negative effect on the relationship, and over a period of time, the almost inevitable result is a serious problem in the relationship.

An essential key for maintaining good relationships in marriage is the kind of attention to the other person in the relationship that produces a sensitivity to the needs and desires of that person. This sensitivity makes it possible to recognize the

signals, sometimes sent unconsciously by a spouse, and to
respond to needs and desires in a way that keeps the relationship developing and improving. Open, honest, and intimate
communication is essential in developing this kind of sensitivity, and it is difficult to imagine this happening apart from time
spent together sharing at the deepest levels. This intimate
knowledge of one another is clearly an important part of the
"one flesh" relationship that is God's intention in marriage.

In trying to resolve the problem created by her failure to
respond quickly to her husband, the beloved expresses her great
appreciation and admiration for her lover in 5:10–16 and, no
doubt, this is one thing that made her seek reconciliation as
quickly and diligently as she did. It is possible that her earlier
failure to respond was in part the result of a lapse in recognizing
the valuable asset that she had in her beloved; it is possible that
she had, if only for a brief moment, come to take him for granted
and this perhaps contributed to her casual response to his overt
signals. Certainly, intimate sharing helps to develop an appreciation for one another that keeps us sensitive and responsive to
the needs and desires of our partner.

2. The Beloved Praises Her Lover (5:9–16)

The beloved's failure to find her lover, despite her search
through the streets of Jerusalem, prompted her to turn to the
daughters of Jerusalem to request their help in finding him and
to instruct them to tell him of her desperate search and desire
("I am lovesick") for him. They begin this section by asking her
what is so special about her lover. Their question is perhaps
prompted by the diligence with which she had been searching
for him and the lengths to which she had gone in her search.
Their question provides her with an opportunity to praise her
lover—the only time in the book she does this—and her praise
reveals to the other women how highly she values her lover, and
this helps to reinforce in her own mind her great esteem and
appreciation for him. It is doubtful that her description of him
was at all helpful to the daughters of Jerusalem in recognizing
her lover although if he actually looked like her description he
certainly would have stood out in a crowd. The description is
what he looked like through the eyes of love.

She begins in verse 10 with a general description of him, and then, beginning with his head and descending to his legs, describes various physical features of her lover. She says that he is radiant, and while the exact meaning of the word used here is uncertain, it perhaps refers to a radiance or shining appearance that was associated with prosperity, strength, and health. In view of her comparisons of him with jewels and precious metals below, it is possible that the word means something like "dazzling" or "shining" here. She next describes him as "ruddy." This word describes a reddish color and it seems likely that the word describes his healthy and vigorous appearance. She concludes this general description of her lover by saying that he is outstanding among ten thousand. In a group of men that size he would surpass them all. In her eyes he was the most outstanding man around and no one else could compare with him.

In verse 11 she describes his head as of "purest gold," emphasizing his great beauty and worth. Next she describes his black hair. The word translated "wavy" occurs only here and it is uncertain whether it refers to the shape of his hair or to its abundance; this uncertainty is evident in the very different ways the word is rendered in the various English translations.

She describes his eyes in verse 12, using the same figure that he used to describe her eyes on two earlier occasions (see the comments on 1:15 and 4:1). Here she adds that his eyes are like doves beside water streams, and this addition seems to add the idea of peace and tranquility to the figure. It is uncertain whether the rest of her description in verse 12 refers to the doves or the eyes and this uncertainty is compounded by the fact that the verse uses a word that occurs only here in the Hebrew Bible. Perhaps the figure is of doves "bathing themselves in milk, perching on a fountain rim" (so reads the Jerusalem Bible). In this case the emphasis would be on the luxury, peacefulness, and perhaps playfulness of his eyes. It seems preferable to understand the last two lines of the verse as describing the eyes rather than the doves and this is the interpretation suggested by the NIV translation, "washed in milk, mounted like jewels." This understanding of the figure emphasizes the color and the brilliant sparkle of the eyes.

In verse 13 she compares his cheeks with a garden of sweet
smelling spices. Despite disagreement about whether one word
in the second line of the verse should be understood as a verbal
form ("yielding") as does NIV and many other translations or as
a noun as does NASB ("banks") and a number of others, the
point of the figure seems clear. It is the pleasant fragrance of the
spices and aromatic ointments to which his cheeks are compared. This may suggest that he used fragrances that were
attractive to her; it may only be indicative of the appeal that his
cheeks had for her. Certain aromas are delightful and appealing
and attractive to another person. Sometimes a wife's special
perfume has that effect, either because of the smell of the
perfume or because the smell is associated with especially
pleasant experiences in the past (perhaps their honeymoon or a
particularly memorable trip or a special Christmas). My wife and
I find the smell of orange and lemon blossoms to be delightful
and sometimes we will just sit in our back yard for a time to
enjoy that lovely aroma. I have gone out of my way to walk
through fields where honeysuckle was blooming along a fence
and have taken far longer than I should to get where I was going
because I found the fragrance of those flowers so stimulating
and enjoyable. It is this kind of delight and attraction that she
finds in the cheeks of her lover.

His lips are compared with lilies dripping with myrrh. The
exact point of her comparison is obscured by the fact that we are
not certain which flower is referred to here. If it is a red or
purplish flower, then the metaphor may describe the color of his
lips; if, as is more likely, it refers to a pale white flower, then the
figure probably emphasizes "softness and beauty."[1] Myrrh was a
costly resin, noted for its fragrance. It was bitter to the taste,[2] so
it seems unlikely that this was a point in the comparison. The
metaphor probably emphasizes the worth of his lips as well as
the appeal and attraction that they held for her. Some have
suggested that this verse describes the speech of the lover; it
seems far more likely, given the context of the Song and its
references to lovemaking, that she is describing his kisses rather
than his speech. The connection of myrrh with lovemaking (see

---

[1] Deere, "Meaning," p. 181.
[2] Ibid.

the comments on 5:5) probably adds force to the comparison as well.

Next his arms, body (or abdomen), legs, and feet are described apparently in the terms of a statue made of gold and precious stones. It is not possible to determine exactly what material is meant in every instance, but the point of the comparison is clear. He is, in his beloved's sight, breathtakingly beautiful, and he is of great worth. His strength is probably emphasized in describing his abdomen as polished ivory and his legs as pillars of marble, though his appearance (strong and muscular) may to some extent be in view as well. His magnificent and breathtaking appearance is again pointed out when he is said to be "like Lebanon, choice as its cedars" in verse 15. All of this simply affirms the point she made at the beginning of this section when she said that he is "outstanding among ten thousand."

It is not clear whether her words in 5:16, "his mouth (actually palate) is sweetness itself," refer to his speech or to his kisses and either would be appropriate here. Her closing comment that he is "altogether lovely" repeats the words that he used to describe her on their wedding night (4:7). She concludes her speech by turning to the daughters of Jerusalem and saying, "This is my lover, this is my friend." One can almost see her standing with hands on her hips as she says these words to the women. It is as if she were saying, "See, I told you he was more outstanding then ten thousand. Do you understand what I mean now?" As Fox suggests, "She speaks in triumphant satisfaction, as if her magnificent verbal creation has irrefutably answered the girls' skepticism."[3]

The great admiration that the girl has for her husband and which he obviously has for her goes a long way toward explaining the relationship that is described in the Song. In this instance, her admiration and appreciation for the great treasure that she has in her husband makes it imperative that she seek reconciliation immediately when a problem arises. Her spouse and their relationship are too important not to expend whatever effort and energy is required to resolve the problem and restore

[3] Fox, *Song of Songs*, p. 149.

their good relationship. It is difficult to imagine the kind of deep and intimate relationship between a husband and wife that is reflected in the Song apart from this kind of mutual appreciation for one another.

The Song clearly reveals the attitude of both partners for each other without explicitly identifying what has produced that mutual appreciation. It would appear that the appreciation and admiration that is an integral part of the excitement of courtship and the "honeymoon" phase of a relationship can continue to grow only in an environment where the strengths of a spouse are focused on rather than weaknesses. There needs to be a conscious and deliberate attempt on the part of each spouse to understand and meet the needs of his or her partner; there needs to be, as well, a conscious recognition of the contribution of the spouse and an explicit acknowledgment of that. My wife has helped me to become a much better husband and person by her loving and appreciative response to even small changes in my behavior and attitudes. This is one important way that we can "spur one another on toward love and good deeds" (Heb. 10:24) in marriage. The application of these principles would transform many marginal marriage relationships into the kind described in the Song where husbands and wives in the loving eyes of their spouses take on the larger than life dimensions that we see in these poems.

3. The Lover Is Found (6:1–3)

The daughters of Jerusalem, presumably convinced that her lover was truly extraordinary, now ask her where he is so that they may help her find him. Her response in 6:2 is surprising and somewhat difficult to understand. In contrast to her earlier search for her lover, she now indicates that he has gone down to his garden. It may be that she has now figured out where he has gone or perhaps someone has informed her apart from what we are told in the text. It is also possible, since 5:2–7 is perhaps a dream, that Deere is correct in his conclusion that her somewhat unexpected answer here "indicates that their separation was more in the emotional realm than in the spatial."[4]

---

[4] Deere, "Meaning," p. 190.

At the very least, the figures she uses have a double meaning, and they strongly suggest that their emotional separation had adversely affected their physical intimacy. The figure of the garden was used earlier (4:12–5:1) of her body, and his going into the garden was used for their sexual intercourse (5:1). She has just described his cheeks as "beds of spices" (5:13). She was described as a lily in 2:1, 2 and the expression "grazing among the lilies" seems to have erotic overtones in 2:16. Finally, the expression "I am my lover's and my lover is mine" is used in a context of desire to make love in 2:16 and 7:10. In view of the associations of almost every word and expression in verses 2 and 3 with either physical intimacy or the desire for it, it is difficult to suppose that the beloved's words here refer only to a literal garden where her offended lover had gone.

4. Reconciliation: The Lover Praises His Beloved (6:4–13)

These verses contain the lover's response to the girl's efforts at reconciliation. His use of many of the phrases that he used in praising her on their wedding night make it clear that he has fully accepted her apology and that she remains his beloved just as she was then. He compares her beauty with that of Tirzah[5] and Jerusalem. Tirzah was located in an area of great natural beauty and was blessed with an abundant water supply, all of which suggests that this was a particularly beautiful city. The mention of Tirzah may also provide a clue that the book was written before the division of the monarchy after the death of Solomon. Tirzah was chosen by Jeroboam I as capital of the Northern Kingdom, and it seems doubtful that a writer from the South after that time would refer to the city in parallel with Jerusalem or that a northern writer would refer to Jerusalem in parallel with Tirzah. The city entered a period of decline after Omri (9th century B.C.) moved the capital of Israel to Samaria. This makes it unlikely that a writer of a late period would use this nonexistent city as a figure for the girl's beauty.

The meaning of the expression translated "majestic as troops with banners" is somewhat obscure, though it probably is

---

[5] The site of the city is generally thought to be Tell el-Farah, northeast of Shechem.

meant to indicate that her elegant beauty produced the same feelings in people as those produced by a splendid army marching in formation.

Glickman has noted that this praise song is somewhat different than the others in the Song because the sensuous and erotic figures that are found in the others are largely missing from this one. He has suggested that this was done by the lover to guard against "the possible misconception that the only reason he wished to make up with her was so he could make love to her."[6] It is likely that his comment in verse 5, "Turn your eyes from me; they overwhelm (or perhaps more likely 'they arouse') me," are to be understood in the light of this observation. The husband wanted to avoid being sexually aroused because he recognized that the restoration of a proper relationship was an important prerequisite to their physical intimacy.

His description of her hair, her teeth, and her temples are almost identical to those found in 4:1–3 and comments about the meaning of the metaphors can be found in the discussion of those verses.

In verses 8 and 9, the lover makes the same point about his beloved that she earlier made about him to the daughters of Jerusalem: He says that there is no one who can compare with her, she is unique. The beloved made her point by comparing her lover with ten thousand other men; her lover makes his point by comparing her with queens and concubines. These women would, no doubt, have reached their coveted positions for a variety of reasons: Some must have been extremely beautiful; others had the right political connections. As a group they represent the ultimate in terms of beauty, wealth, power, the best families, etc. In comparison with these women, she surpasses them all. Despite their disagreement, there is no one to whom he would rather be married; she remains his unique and precious one. He even goes on to say that she is so outstanding that the daughters (that is the meaning of the word translated "maidens," NIV), queens, and concubines praise her.

The offended lover's response to the apology of his wife is both interesting and significant. He clearly accepts his beloved's

---

[6]Glickman, *Song for Lovers*, p. 72.

obvious but, in the text at least, not explicit apology. He does it by praising her in such a way as to make it clear that he loves her with the same excitement that was the case on their honeymoon. There is no mention of her offense in his response; he does not in any way upbraid in accepting her apology. People sometimes accept apologies from those who have offended them in a way that humiliates and demeans and that seems to constitute a greater wrong than was done to them in the first place. It is difficult, if not impossible, to build and maintain excellent relationships apart from the kind of gracious acceptance that is reflected in this lover's response.

It is difficult to determine the speaker of the words in verse 10. Since the words, "Who is this?" at the beginning of verse 10 are used elsewhere in the book (3:6 and 8:5) by a third party such as the daughters of Jerusalem, it is possible that this is the case here. Verse 10 may be a statement of praise for the girl offered by the women mentioned in verse 9. It could also be their response to the extravagant praise that the lover had for the girl, and they may be asking, "Who could ever measure up to that kind of praise?" On the other hand, the last line of verse 10 repeats exactly the last phrase of verse 4 (despite the curious fact that NIV translates the difficult phrase in two very different ways in the two verses), and this suggests that the lover may be speaking in verse 10. Despite the uncertainty as to who is speaking here, the praise for the girl is obvious.

Verse 11 appears to be the beloved's account of the reconciliation. She had determined in 6:2 that her lover had gone to his garden, and this verse indicates that she went to the nut grove to see the condition of the plants there. This may indicate that the garden and the nut grove were actual places, but as was the case in 6:2, there is a figurative meaning of the expressions that relates to the condition of their relationship. Their relationship was described in similar terms in 2:10–13, 15 and 4:12, 13; it will be described in these same terms again in 7:11–12.

Verse 12 is acknowledged by commentators as perhaps the most obscure verse in the Song and one of the most difficult in the entire Bible. It apparently describes her surprise at encountering her lover unexpectedly and at the ease with which their reconciliation was accomplished. Presumably his setting her among the royal chariots (if that is the correct translation of the Hebrew phrase) refers to her restoration to her previous place beside the king.

The plural form used in the first half of verse 13 ("that *we* may gaze on you") identify these as words, most likely, from the daughters of Jerusalem. They appear to be calling the girl back from the nut garden where she had gone to look for her lover. The last part of verse 13 seems to be the lover's response to the women who had spoken to the girl, and his words are a comment on their intense interest in seeing this beautiful girl. At the same time his words imply that in their now restored relationship her proper place is with her lover. It is as if the two are standing together reconciled and they hear the words of the women calling the girl to return to them. He turns to them and says, in effect, "Do not disturb us with your request to gaze on her; I am the one who properly should enjoy her beauty." He then turns to his beloved in 7:1–9 and praises her in perhaps the most sensuous terms found in the Song. Her response to his words (7:9b–13), "Let us go to the countryside . . . there I will give you my love," seems to support this understanding as well.

The girl is referred to in this verse as "the Shulammite," and this term has produced considerable discussion. Some have understood it as indicating where she was from, and since no place called Shulem is known, it has been suggested that this is a variant of the name Shunem, the home city of Abishag, the girl who provided body heat to David in his illness when he was old (1 Kings 1:1–4). Some have supposed that the girl described in the Song is, in fact, Abishag and that this explains Solomon's great anger when Adonijah requested that Abishag be given to him (1 Kings 2:15–25).

Some have suggested that the name is related to the Hebrew root from which *shalom*, "peace," comes and that Shulammite means something like "the peaceable one" or the "perfect, unblemished one." A third possibility is suggested by the fact that the word seems to be a feminine form of the name Solomon. This would work very well if the term Solomon was meant to be a kind of generic designation for a groom; Shulammite would be the corresponding designation for the bride. One problem for this view is that the word "Shulammite" occurs with the Hebrew definite article while proper names, including the name Solomon throughout this book, never occur with the article. Thus, the term could not be an exact counterpart to the name Solomon; it would have to mean something like "Solomon's lady." It is difficult to decide among these views because none are without problems.

A second uncertainty in this verse involves the meaning of the "dance of Mahanaim." The Hebrew word *mahanaim* means "two camps" and is the name Jacob gave to the place where he saw a group of angels opposite his camp in Genesis 32:2. It is not clear whether the word here means "two camps/groups" or refers to the place in Gilead. Nor do we have any information about that place to provide a clue for determining what the dance was. The only basis for making this decision has to come from the context of this passage and the book of Song of Songs. The suggestions that have been made are little more than speculation. Some have suggested that this was a dance performed at wedding ceremonies (a sword dance or a seductive dance) either by the bride or by the guests. Some have suggested that it was a dance performed by the girl for her husband, though it should be noted that the text does not connect this with a wedding nor does it say that the girl did the dance. It only says that the women would look at the girl like one would look at the dance of Mahanaim. It is impossible, without further information, to say more about this dance than that whatever it was, it caused people to watch the dancing very intently.

For Further Study

1. Why do you think the girl delayed in responding to her lover's needs/desires? What contributes to this attitude in a marriage relationship? What can be done to keep this from happening?

2. What does the incident about the couple's separation suggest about the importance of responding to the needs/desires of your spouse? What can you do to become more aware of your mate's needs? When was the last time you went out of your way to do something special for your husband/wife?

3. The praise of one lover for the other is a common element in every section of the Song. What do you think is the significance of this?

4. How does the beloved's attitude toward her lover, as seen in 5:10–16, affect her determination to resolve their problems? How can this attitude be preserved through the years of marriage?

Chapter 10

Moving Toward Maturity, Part 2
(7:1–8:4)

B. The Relationship Restored (7:1–8:4)

Some have suggested that all of 6:13 is spoken by the onlookers at the wedding and that they are calling for her to dance for them.[1] It is then suggested that 7:1–5 are spoken by the same group of people as they watch her dance, and it is argued that the plural form in 6:13 and the reference to the king in the third person in 7:5 support this understanding of the passage. It seems far more likely (and most commentators concur in this) that the last half of 6:13 is the lover's reply to the women who called to the Shulammite to return to them. After he addresses these women, he turns to his beloved, with whom he has been reconciled, and he praises her beauty in 7:1–9a.

There are clear parallels between this section and 4:1–5:1. In both there is a poem in praise of the beauty of the beloved (4:1–7 and 7:1–6), and this is followed by a statement of desire on the part of the lover to enjoy the pleasures of her love (4:8–15 and 7:7–9a). The beloved then responds with an invitation to enjoy love together (4:16 and 7:9b–13).

1. Praise for the Beloved and Her Love (7:1–9a)

These verses constitute another *wasaf* or praise song by the lover. He praises her physical beauty, beginning with her feet and moving upward to her head. He uses metaphors that suggest wealth, beauty, abundance, fine craftsmanship, etc. Her exqui-

---

[1] E.g., Carr, TOTC, p. 156.

site beauty, her noble and majestic appearance, and her great
value in his eyes are emphasized. The repetition of the
expression "How beautiful" in verses 1 and 6 suggests that
these verses constitute the praise section of his words, while
verses 7–9a contain his expression of desire to share her love.
Verse 7 provides a summary of his praise for her and it is
difficult to decide whether it belongs with the first section of his
speech or with the second.

He begins by praising her "sandaled feet." Since he ends
his praise of her in verse 5 with her head and hair, this may be
his way of saying, "From the soles of your feet to the top of your
head, you are beautiful." It is also possible that he finds
extremely beautiful even parts of her such as her feet, which
would normally not be thought attractive. There is a possible
parallel to this in the apocryphal book of Judith 16:8–9. That
passage celebrates a great victory over Israel's enemies, and the
victory was effected by Judith using her great beauty to lure the
enemy leader into a situation where she could kill him. The
verse says, "Her sandal ravished his eye, her beauty captured
his soul, and the sword severed his neck." It has been suggested
from this that "the sandal left the top of the foot virtually bare
and this was apparently regarded as especially captivating."[2]

Her "graceful legs" are described as "like jewels, the work
of a craftsman's hands." The Hebrew expression seems to mean
the "curves of the thighs," and they are described as beautiful
ornaments or jewels (the Hebrew word occurs only here in the
Hebrew Bible) that have been made by a master craftsman. The
reference to her as "prince's daughter" refers to her noble
beauty (or character) rather than to her family background.

In verse 3, her navel is described as "a rounded goblet that
never lacks blended wine." A number of commentators have
argued that the sequence of body parts described moves
systematically upward, and since her waist or belly is described
next, this must refer to something below her waist. Many of
these commentators conclude that a sensual poem like this
would not omit reference to the female genitals and suspect, on
the basis of an Arabic cognate, that this is a description of the

---

[2] Pope, AB, p. 614. The translation from Judith is also from Pope.

beloved's vulva.[3] Actually, the Hebrew word translated by NIV "waist" means "abdomen or belly," and this would not necessarily be below the navel since the word refers to the larger area where the navel is located. Fox has pointed out that the ascending order is not strictly adhered to throughout, since "the eyes are not lower than the item mentioned after them, the nose (v. 5b), nor is the head (v. 6a) higher than they."[4] Since the meaning "navel" is clearly attested for this Hebrew word, and since that meaning makes perfectly good sense here, there seems to be no good reason for rejecting that as the correct meaning in this verse.[5]

The mention of her navel as an item for praise may, as Fox suggests, indicate that "the navel was considered pretty (as it is in the *Arabian Nights*),"[6] though Deere is probably correct in suggesting that the point of comparing her navel with a goblet constantly filled with mixed wine lies less in the realm of the visual than in the realm of taste, desirability, and function. He says, "The sense of taste inherent in the wine metaphor probably indicated the Lover's desire to kiss the abdomen of the Beloved. Her body was as desirable and intoxicating as wine."[7] Her "waist" (better "abdomen") is compared with "a mound of wheat surrounded by lilies." Perhaps this refers to the gentle curvature of her abdomen or to its color. Deere suggests that the point of the comparison is found in the function of wheat. For the lover, the beloved is both food (wheat) and drink (wine).[8] He also suggests that the joy that accompanied the completion of harvest (a mound of grain) may be communicated through the metaphor as well. It is often suggested that fences of thorns

---

[3] E.g., Carr, TOTC, p. 157 and Pope, AB, p. 617.

[4] Fox, *Song*, p. 159.

[5] Deere ("Meaning," p. 200) also correctly notes that underlying the interpretation of at least some of these commentators is the opinion that the sensuality of the Song is far more overt and explicit than it is. The Song, and especially this poem, is sensual, but as Deere says, "The style of the Song is much too delicate and metaphorical to admit to such a crass interpretation" as is suggested by many today. The Song resembles the Egyptian love poetry in this regard, and both stand in strong contrast to the Ugaritic/Canaanite and Mesopotamian material, which is quite explicit in its language.

[6] Fox, *Song*, p. 159.

[7] Deere, "Meaning," p. 202.

[8] Ibid., p. 203.

were put around mounds of harvested grain to protect it from animals and perhaps this is what lies behind the statement that the mound of wheat is fenced or encircled with lilies. Thus, the harshness of the expected fence of thorns is replaced by the beauty of lilies. It is possible that the earlier description of the lover browsing among the lilies (2:16 and 7:3) adds force to the metaphor.

His description of her breasts as fawns repeats his words in 4:5. For the meaning of the metaphor, see the discussion of that verse.

Her neck is described in verse 4 as "like an ivory tower." A number of ivory carvings have been found in excavations of ancient palaces (The ivories from Samaria and from Ugarit are especially beautiful examples.), and it is probably articles like these that were in the mind of the lover as he described the neck of his beloved. The figure probably emphasizes her elegant and exquisite beauty, and the delicate workmanship that he sees reflected in the smoothness of her neck. It is possible that the color of ivory is in view here as, no doubt, is its value and desirability.

Her eyes are described as "the pools of Heshbon," and as Carr suggests, "The sense here is one of still, deep calmness rather than the sparkle and shimmer of flowing springs."[9] Excavations at Heshbon, an Ammonite royal city, have revealed "the ruins of a huge reservoir of excellent masonry . . . in the valley at the foot of the hill where the town stood,"[10] and something like this may have been in view as the figure was used. The location of the gate of Bath Rabbim is not known.

The description of her nose as "the tower of Lebanon looking toward Damascus" does not strike the modern reader as a compliment, and commentators have struggled with the meaning of this metaphor perhaps more than any other in the Song. Part of the difficulty comes from our not knowing what "the tower of Lebanon" refers to. It has been suggested that it was a military outpost or the Lebanon mountain range or a tower on top of one of the mountains. It has been suggested that the tower "was celebrated for its great symmetry and elegance" and

---

[9]Carr, TOTC, p. 158.
[10]Pope, AB, p. 625.

that it is a figure for her "well proportioned nose."[11] Carr has suggested that it was white cliffs that gave Mt. Lebanon its name (The Hebrew words "Lebanon" and "white" are similar.), and that the point of this comparison is found in the color rather than the size or shape of her nose.[12] The Hebrew word "frankincense" is also similar to the word Lebanon, and there is perhaps a connection between both the color white, the fragrance of frankincense, and the meaning of this metaphor. Others have suggested that it is her stately appearance or her strong character or her beauty that is emphasized by the comparison.

Mt. Carmel is a prominent mountain that blocks passage between northern and southern Israel. It is a majestic and beautiful mountain, and the girl's head is compared with this mountain to emphasize her majestic beauty and her impressive appearance.

Her hair (The Hebrew word suggests that her hair hangs loosely and freely.) is like purple (In NIV, "royal tapestry" is an attempt to convey the connotations of the Hebrew word.). It is unlikely that the point of this comparison lies in the realm of color since this color, obtained from the murex shellfish, ranges from what we call purple to deep crimson; rather, the point comes from the fact that this particular color was very expensive and commonly used by royalty. The lover praises his beloved by using a metaphor that emphasized royalty and worth. He concludes his description by noting the effect that her hair has on him—"a king is held captive by the tresses."

Verse 6 ends the section as it began with the words, "How beautiful," and he praises both her beauty and the delights of her love in this verse.

Verse 7 looks back to the lover's praise for the girl and summarizes that praise; at the same time it looks forward and constitutes the introduction to his expression of desire for her. Her stature (The Hebrew word normally means "height.") is compared to a date palm tree and her breasts to the clusters of dates. The comparison here is almost certainly to the sweetness of the dates, and the lover is expressing his desire to taste or kiss her breasts. His intention is made clear in verse 8, when he says,

---

[11]Ginsburg, *Song*, p. 179.

[12]Carr, TOTC, p. 159. Note also the comparison of her neck to ivory in v. 4.

"I will climb the palm tree, I will take hold of its fruit." In the second half of verse 8 the figure changes from clusters of dates to clusters of grapes, another sweet and delectable fruit. He compares the fragrance of her breath[13] with apples, or more likely apricots, and her mouth with the best wine. He compares her with a variety of delicious and delightful delicacies and obviously his desire is to enjoy to the full the delights of her love.

2. The Beloved's Response and Invitation (7:9b–13)

The fact that the beloved is being addressed in verses 2–9a is clear because of the feminine suffixes that are used. That the girl begins to speak after the first line of verse 9 is indicated by the words translated "my lover," the usual name by which the girl refers to the lover, and by the words "I belong to my lover" in verse 10, words that she has used in similar circumstances in 2:16 and 6:3. As was the case in 4:16, she picks up the figures that he has been using and invites him to share her love.

The translation of the last word in verse 9 is uncertain. The present Hebrew text is reflected in the translation of the NASB, "Flowing gently *through* the lips of those who fall asleep." If this reading is correct, it pictures, as Glickman suggests, "the closeness of a couple falling asleep in each other's arms"[14] after their lovemaking. Most modern commentators follow a reading suggested by several ancient versions and change one letter of the present Hebrew text. The result of this is a reading that many feel is more in harmony with the context and the figures that are being used. This slight change is reflected in the NIV translation, "flowing gently over lips and teeth."

Verse 10 is especially interesting because of its use of the word translated "desire." Besides this passage, the word occurs in the Old Testament only in Genesis 3:16 and 4:7, and there its

---

[13]The Hebrew word translated "breath" normally means "nose" rather than "breath." It is possible that it does mean "breath" here since the nose is the organ of breathing. It is also possible that this verse (and perhaps 7:2 as well) refers to the custom of nose kissing. Fox (*Song*, p. 97) says that "A gesture of affection in the ancient East . . . was the nose kiss, in which the couple would rub faces together and smell each other's nose." He goes on to say that "the most intimate and sensual kiss was the mouth kiss."

[14]Glickman, *Song*, p. 86.

meaning seems to be "a desire to dominate or rule over." Here the desire is obviously sexual. The significance of the passage lies in the fact that Genesis 3:16 deals with the relationship between the man and woman and is part of the curse that resulted from the Fall. This part of the curse was addressed to the woman and says, "Your desire shall be for your husband; he shall rule over you." The verse suggests that the relationship between the man and woman changed after the Fall. Her desire was to dominate him and rule over him rather than submit to his loving leadership. At the same time, the man's leadership changed from a gentle loving leadership to a dominating and often tyrannical rule.[15]

Both the use of the word "desire" and the extensive use of the garden imagery throughout Song of Songs suggests that there is a relationship between this passage and Genesis 3. In this verse the beloved says that her lover's desire is for her—the opposite of the situation described in the curse. Even though the "desire" seems to be somewhat different than in Genesis 3:16, the implication of the verse is that in an ideal relationship between a man and a woman, there can be a negation of some of the adverse effects of the curse. It is possible that her statement "I belong to my lover" acknowledges his headship in their relationship. In any case, it is clear that in this ideal relationship between the lover and his beloved, a very different spirit prevails than is reflected in Genesis 3:16; it reflects the same kind of positive potential for marriage that Paul affirms in Ephesians 5:22–33 and elsewhere.

The beloved's invitation to her lover is found in verses 11–13, and the point of her invitation is clear: "I will give you my love. . . . every delicacy . . . that I have stored up for you." Again the figures of gardens and budding plants are used. Pomegranates and mandrakes, both of which are associated with love and lovemaking, are specifically mentioned. Their maturing relationship is described in terms of spring, just as it was before their marriage. As Deere notes, "spring is a universal symbol for the transformation of life that takes place when a couple falls in

---

[15] For a justification of this interpretation of Gen. 3:16 see Susan T. Foh, "What is the Woman's Desire?" *Westminster Theological Journal*, 37 (1975), 376–83.

love. The beloved uses this image to ask whether there was still the same freshness and anticipation that had initially characterized their relationship."[16] It seems clear that the answer to her question is Yes. Their relationship, as it matures, continues to grow in its freshness and excitement.

3. The Beloved's Desire (8:1–4)

It is likely that the scene has changed from the previous verses, and it is possible that the two are together in the countryside in response to her suggestion. It is possible, as well, that the two are in one another's arms (verse 3) as the beloved speaks these words. In verse 1 she expresses her wish that he were her brother. The lover has referred to her as his "sister" (4:9 and 5:1), and this was common in Egypt as well (e.g., in the love poems translated by White). The key to understanding what the girl means may be found in some sort of cultural taboo against showing affection in public except between blood relatives. As Carr suggests, "What was not in good taste even for a husband and wife was perfectly permissible for a brother and sister."[17] The continuation of her words in verse 1 makes it clear that the wish that he were her brother is related to her desire to be able to kiss him in public without it being considered inappropriate.

She sees their relationship in a number of different aspects in these verses. As a brother she could kiss him in public; as a little brother, she could lead him to her mother's house. She would there serve as his hostess by serving him wine. There seems to be a deliberate ambiguity in verse 2 in the words translated "she who has taught me." The Hebrew verb can be understood as either a third person feminine form, "she teaches me," in which case it would refer to the girl's mother. It can also be understood as a second person masculine form, "you teach me," in which case it would refer to the lover teaching the girl. This is perhaps an example of the kind of playful ambiguity that often characterizes words between two lovers. The relationship viewed under various aspects finally focuses on their relation-

---

[16] Deere, "Meaning," p. 213.

[17] Carr, TOTC, p. 166. See also Deere ("Meaning," p. 215) for other examples of similar customs.

ship as lovers, and her serving him pomegranate wine moves into an expression of her desire to be embraced by her lover.

Her words in verse 3 are the same words that she used in 2:6, and her words are followed by an almost identical exhortation to the daughters of Jerusalem both here and in 2:7 (The exhortation, in identical words to 2:7, also occurs in 3:5.). The differences in form between the two exhortations is not considered to be significant by most interpreters, and thus this verse is translated in the same way as 2:7 and 3:5 in most English translations (but see the marginal note in NASB). It may well be, however, that the difference in form is significant here. The Hebrew expression used in 8:4 would normally be translated either "Why would you arouse . . . love" or "How could you arouse . . . *this kind of* love?" It is the fact that it so nearly repeats the earlier exhortation to the daughters of Jerusalem and repeats it in an almost identical context that prompts interpreters to suppose that 8:4 is simply a restatement of the earlier exhortations.

It seems to the present author that the development of the plot to this point provides a justification for supposing that the difference in form is significant and that the correct translation of the Hebrew interrogative particle (or Hebrew prefix that indicates a question) is either "why" or "how."

We have suggested that the relationship between the lover and the beloved has progressed throughout the course of the book. Chapter 2:6–7 describes a time early in their relationship where her love for her lover creates in her a strong desire for physical intimacy with him. That desire cannot be appropriately realized because they are not yet married. The exhortation comes to remind the girls of Jerusalem that love like they see between the king and his beloved cannot be forced despite the desirability and appeal of such a relationship; it also serves as a reminder to her that her desire for intimacy could not be appropriately realized in the circumstances that then prevailed. Chapter 3:4–5 also occurs before the couple is married and it too comes in a context where the girl's love for her lover causes her to desire strongly sexual intimacy with him. Again the exhortation of 3:5 warns the girls that love between two people cannot be forced and serves as a reminder to her that her desire for the full physical expression of their love must wait until after they are married.

The exhortation of 8:4 comes in a different context: The girl and her lover are now married, and their desire for sexual intimacy has become a reality. Their sexual relationship is seen, however, as only one manifestation of a relationship that is continuing to become deeper and more mature. The section that preceded these verses described one episode in which the lovers' delight in one another led them to enjoy the full physical expression of their love. It seems likely that this exhortation to the daughters of Jerusalem comes as the two lovers are embracing (8:3). The point of the exhortation is to affirm what has been suggested before by the exhortation—the kind of relationship that this book follows from courtship to maturity cannot be forced or hurried into existence. Now that the relationship has been seen in all its intimacy and delight, the girl is saying to the daughters of Jerusalem by the slightly different form of adjuration, "I charge you, 'How could you arouse or awake this kind of love until it so desires.' "[18] The next section then describes the nature of the true love that has been depicted in this book.

For Further Study

1. When was the last time you praised your husband/wife in the way reflected in this section of the Song? When was the last time you expressed your appreciation to your spouse for what they do for you or just for marrying you?

2. Do you think there is a connection between the praise and encouragement for one another found throughout the Song and the delight and excitement for each other that characterizes the relationship between these lovers?

3. What do you do for your husband/wife to show them that you care for and appreciate them? Is it possible to communicate that to them through means other than words? Can words unsupported by deeds communicate this to your mate?

---

[18]Carr (TOTC, p. 168), following a suggestion made by J. Cheryl Exum, concludes that the refrain is now, "Why do you rouse and waken love?" The context makes it clear that this has already happened and there is no need for any further stimulation from the onlookers.

Chapter 11

The Nature of Love and the Lover's Reflection

(8:5–14)

C. The Nature of True Love (8:5–7)

These verses are recognized by virtually all commentators as the climax of the book. The relationship between the lover and his beloved has been described from a number of vantage points, and the excitement and desirability of this kind of relationship is clearly evident. The book has affirmed through the repetition of the refrain of 8:4 at several different points in the development of the relationship that this kind of relationship cannot be forced; it must be allowed to develop naturally.[1] These verses make some important observations about the nature of love as an appropriate extension of the point that has just been reaffirmed through the refrain. The book has to this point simply presented various pictures of the developing relationship between the lovers. These verses, in a way that is somewhat unusual for the Old Testament, draw abstract principles from the story that has been related.

In both instances where the refrain of 8:4 has been encountered previously in the book, it has been followed by the appearance of the lover (2:8 and 3:6 [where it is perhaps the beloved who appears]). In this instance it is the couple who appear together following the refrain, and she tells him, "Under the apple tree I roused you." Her use of the word "roused" clearly seems to tie this verse to the refrain where the daughters

---

[1] As White (*Language of Love*, p. 141) notes about the refrain, "This frequent repetition comments on the nature of love itself: it is a delight that must happen in its own time and should not be prodded unnecessarily."

of Jerusalem were urged not to rouse love. What the daughters of Jerusalem could not do in the love relationship between the lover and the beloved, the beloved was able to accomplish. The reference to the apple tree and to his mother's giving birth to him is difficult and has posed major problems for interpreters. Perhaps it is best to understand the verse symbolically, and to suppose that the girl is comparing the beginning of their love relationship (The apple or apricot tree was a well-known symbol for love in the ancient Near East.) with the birth process. Just as the lover's physical life began with his mother conceiving him (through an act of love), so their love began when she aroused or awakened love in him. Love is not without its trauma and pain and struggle, and that has clearly been a part of the development of the relationship described here; thus, it can be appropriately compared with the birth process.

In 8:6 she requests that she be placed like a seal over her lover's heart or like a seal on his arm. The idea of closeness to him is certainly one point in her use of this metaphor since the seal would be carried on a cord around a person's neck or would be worn as a ring on the hand (Probably "arm" is simply a poetic synonym for hand here.). Seals were used in the ancient world as an indication of ownership. The seal was seen as an extension of the authority of an individual. Joseph was given the signet ring of the pharaoh and thus had his authority; the same idea is found in the Book of Esther with the signet ring of the Persian king, and it was a particularly valuable possession of an individual. This metaphor probably conveys her desire to be identified with her lover in the closest possible way and to be an extension of him in the conduct of his affairs.

By stating that love is as strong as death, the point is made that it is both persistent and irresistible. Even as love cannot be forced, neither can it be resisted when it begins to develop between two people. Love is relentless, and it has the power to overcome obstacles of all kinds.

Love has a strong and possessive character. Love is exclusive and refuses to give up the one loved. It is jealous and as unwilling to surrender the one loved as Sheol is to give up those who belong to her. This jealousy is the same characteristic that is frequently associated with God; it is His demand that His people (His by virtue of creation, His covenant, and His redemption of them) worship and serve Him exclusively. Likewise, true love is intolerant of rivals; it gives an exclusive commitment to another and it expects that same kind of commitment in return. That expectation is as intense as the flames of a raging fire.

It is unclear whether the Hebrew should be translated "mighty flame" (NIV) or "the *very* flame of the LORD" (NASB). If NASB is correct, the verse perhaps implies that this appropriate jealousy (as opposed to the almost pathological suspicion and mistrust that is sometimes a disruptive force in relationships) has its origins with the LORD and is a part of His design in this kind of relationship between a man and a woman. As Deere suggests, "The love of the Song is universal and irresistible like death, exclusive and possessive like Sheol, passionate and invincible against the forces of time and eternity because it is supported by the Creator of all power."[2] In view of this description of love—a description based on the relationship described in the book—one wonders whether this could describe a relationship that Solomon actually experienced. It would appear that these statements about the exclusive nature of the commitment involved precludes that possibility. Certainly Solomon's experiences and disappointments in this area would have served him well for writing this book about the potential that exists for love between a man and a woman, but one can question, given what we know about his harem, whether this kind of relationship was ever experienced by him.

Verse 7 continues the image of love as a fire and indicates that "many waters cannot quench love," and the parallelism adds that "rivers cannot wash it away." As Carr says, "The tenacious staying power of love is set against these tides and perennial rivers which are unable either to wash love away or to put out its sparks."[3] The basic point of this figure is obvious, but in the light of associations elsewhere of water, deep water, flood, and deep with personal danger and with cosmic forces that threaten the order and stability of the world (e.g., Job 38:8–11), it is possible that the section is suggesting something else. It is

---

[2] Deere, "Meaning," p. 231.
[3] Carr, TOTC, p. 171.

possible that the section is saying that the cosmic forces of chaos
and disorder—the same forces that were responsible for the Fall
and the resulting disharmony between the man and the
woman—can be to a certain extent overcome by the power of
the kind of love described in the Song, a love that comes
ultimately from the LORD and His design.

The last part of verse 7 extends the idea that love cannot be
forced, an idea that has been repeated in the refrain of 2:7, 3:5,
and 8:4, and makes a point that must have been painfully
obvious to Solomon. The verse affirms that love cannot be
bought. A person can give all the money that he has but he can
never buy love; he can buy sex, he can buy companionship, he
could, no doubt, even buy a wife, but he cannot buy love. Love
is something that, by its very nature, must be given freely.

D. The Couple's Reflection and Response (8:8–14)

This concluding section of the Song is often treated by
commentators as if it were only an unnecessary appendage to
the book, which reached its climax in 8:5–7. These last verses
are not characterized by the difficult vocabulary that is encountered in almost every verse of the Song; nevertheless, the exact
meaning of the figures and the identity of the speakers makes
the interpretation of the section difficult.

The plural forms of "we" in verses 8 and 9 at least make it
clear that a group is speaking here. It seems likely that the
speakers are the brothers who were mentioned in 1:6 and who
play something of an adversary role in the story. It is known that
the brothers often played a role in working out the arrangements
for marriage contracts (e.g., Dinah's brothers in Gen. 34 and
Rebekah's brother in Gen. 24), and a part of that probably
involved giving permission to the girl when they approved of
the groom, negotiating the details of the bride price, etc. A part
of that would also likely involve their determination about
whether their sister was ready for marriage. It seems likely that
verses 8–10 recall a conversation about the girl's readiness for
marriage that took place between the girl and her brothers prior
to her marriage. This section not only illustrates the fact that
love is something that is freely given (v. 12), it also illustrates
another of the obstacles that was encountered in their relation-

ship—the obstacle of her brothers' resistance to their sister's relationship with her lover.

Verse 8 seems to indicate the brothers' desire to do what is appropriate for their sister when the time for her marriage comes, and verse 9, while taken by most to indicate how the brothers will prepare their sister before the time of her marriage (The wall is taken as symbolic of chastity; the door of promiscuity.), seems to be a continuation of the idea begun in verse 8. The exact meaning of "wall" and "door" is not clear but the verse appears to describe the elaborate adornment[4] that the brothers intended to provide for their sister when she was old enough for marriage; now they consider her too young, since "her breasts are not yet grown."

The girl's reply to her brothers in verse 10 reveals a substantial disagreement with the brothers' assessment of the situation. She says, and one would imagine rather defiantly, "I am a wall, and my breasts are like towers." In her opinion she has all the adornment that she needs for marriage and she is sufficiently mature as well. She points out to them in a somewhat ambiguous statement that the king shares her opinion. She has become "in his eyes like one bringing contentment" (or like one finding peace or contentment).

It is difficult to decide whether the word translated "bringing" is best understood in that way, or as another word which means "finding" (as in NASB) since the same Hebrew word can be understood either way. The exact nuance of the Hebrew word "peace" (*shalom*) is uncertain here. The basic meaning of the word has to do with being whole or complete and thus the phrase can describe her as one who is in the king's eyes "complete" in the sense of being sufficiently mature for marriage or it can refer to the fact that she brings him (or has found) contentment. It is also possible that this expression is a variation of the common Hebrew expression "to find favor in one's eyes," and that she is saying that irregardless of what the

---

[4]As Fox (*Song*, p. 173) points out, the Hebrew word translated "door" is the solid object that bars entry. If this was meant to symbolize "entry and promiscuity," it seems likely that the word indicating the opening of the doorway would have been used. Fox further points out that cedar would not be used to barricade the girl; its use was primarily for decoration rather than security.

brothers think, her lover finds her perfectly mature and acceptable. The basic meaning of her reply to her brothers is not
changed regardless of the decisions made about this perhaps
intentionally ambiguous phrase. Some have suggested that in
the ambiguity there is a deliberate play on the words "Shulammite," "Solomon," and "peace"—all of which are related to the
same Hebrew root. The girl is saying, "The Shulammite is
bringing peace/contentment to Solomon," and perhaps con-
versely, "The Shulammite has found peace/contentment in
Solomon."

As Deere notes about verses 11 and 12, "This small unit
(8:11–12) is one of the more enigmatic portions of the Song and
numerous theories have been advanced to explain it."[5] In spite
of the interpretive difficulties, it is clear that the beloved is
speaking in verse 12 and that her own vineyard is her own body
or person. It is also clear from verse 11 that the thousand shekels
of silver is the owner's portion from the production of the
vineyard. The beloved is saying that she is willingly giving to
Solomon the owner's share from her own vineyard. The book
has emphasized that love cannot be forced or bought; it must be
given freely and that is precisely what happened in the ideal
relationship that has been described in the Song. It is not clear
whether the caretakers of the beloved's vineyard are her
brothers who, despite her differences with them, prepared and
protected her for marriage or whether she is the caretaker of her
own vineyard (in contrast to the situation she noted in 1:6).

Verse 13 is spoken by the lover to his beloved, and he
addresses her as "the one sitting in the garden." He tells her
that there are others—the Hebrew word means "companions"
and it is not clear to whom it refers, though it cannot refer
exclusively to the daughters of Jerusalem because it is a
masculine plural form—listening to what she is saying.[6] The
lover expresses his desire that he alone may hear her voice. She
responds in verse 14 with words that previously have been
associated with the desire for intimacy (2:9, 17, and 4:6). The
implication is that the two lovers leave their "companions" to be

---

[5] Deere, "Meaning," p. 236.
[6] The Hebrew word used here means "to listen, to pay attention," and NASB
("listening") seems preferable to NIV ("in attendance") here.

alone together. Thus, the book ends with the relationship that we have followed from its earliest stages through its development into a deep and mature love continuing to deepen further as the lovers share their lives together.

For Further Study

1. Reflect on the excitement, freshness, and delight that were part of your relationship with your husband/wife when you were first married. Does that still characterize your relationship? What lessons can you learn from Song of Songs that might restore that excitement and appreciation for your mate?

2. Both the positive and the negative potential in marriage relationships is recognized in passages like Proverbs 12:4; 14:1; 18:22; 21:9, 19 and 27:15–16. How can the instruction of Song of Solomon be applied to realize the positive possibilities that marriage offers?

Bibliography

Allen, Ronald B. *Praise! A Matter of Life and Breath*. Nashville, Tennessee: Thomas Nelson Publishers, 1978.

Archer, Gleason L., Jr. *A Survey of Old Testament Introduction*. Chicago: Moody Press, 1964.

Bullock, G. Hassel. *An Introduction to the Poetic Books of the Old Testament*. Chicago: Moody Press, 1972.

Campbell, Edward. *Ruth*. The Anchor Bible. Garden City, New York: Doubleday & Company, 1975.

Carr, G. L. *The Song of Songs*. Tyndale Old Testament Commentaries. Downers Grove, Illinois: InterVarsity Press, 1984.

Curtis, Edward M. "Old Testament Wisdom: A Model for Faith-Learning Integration." *Christian Scholar's Review*, XV (1986), 213–27.

Deere, Jack S. "The Meaning of the Song of Songs: An Historical and Exegetical Inquiry." Unpublished Th.D. dissertation, Dallas Theological Seminary, 1984.

Delitzsch, Franz. *A Commentary on the Song of Songs*. Translated by M. G. Easton. Grand Rapids, Michigan: Wm. B. Eerdmans Publishing Company, 1950.

Falk, Marcia. *Love Lyrics from the Bible*. Sheffield: The Almond Press, 1982.

Fox, Michael V. *The Song of Songs and the Ancient Egyptian Love Songs*. Madison, Wisconsin: The University of Wisconsin Press, 1985.

Ginsburg, Christian D. *The Song of Songs and Coholeth*. With a Prolegomenon by Sheldon Blank. New York: KTAV Publishing House, 1857. Reprinted with new material 1970.

Glickman, S. Craig. *A Song for Lovers*. Downers Grove, Illinois: InterVarsity Press, 1976.

Godet, F. "The Interpretation of the Song of Songs." *Classical Evangelical Essays in Old Testament Interpretation*. Edited by Walter Kaiser, Jr. Grand Rapids, Michigan: Baker Book House, 1972.

Gordis, Robert. *The Song of Songs and Lamentations*. New York: KTAV Publishing House, Revised and augmented 1974.

Landy, Francis. "Beauty and the Enigma: An Inquiry into Some Interrelated Episodes of the Song of Songs." *Journal for the Study of the Old Testament*, 17 (1980), 55–106.

Pope, Marvin H. *Song of Songs*. The Anchor Bible. Garden City, New York: Doubleday & Company, 1977.

Rowley, H. H. "The Interpretation of the Song of Songs." *The Servant of the Lord and Other Essays on the Old Testament*. Oxford: Blackwell, 1965.

White, John B. *A Study of the Language of Love in the Song of Songs and Ancient Egyptian Love Poetry*. Society of Biblical Literature Dissertation Series 38. Missoula, Montana: Scholar's Press, 1978.

Wright, J. Stafford. "The Interpretation of Ecclesiastes." *Classical Evangelical Essays in Old Testament Interpretation*. Edited by Walter Kaiser, Jr. Grand Rapids, Michigan: Baker Book House, 1972.

Young, Edward J. *An Introduction to the Old Testament*. Grand Rapids, Michigan: Wm. B. Eerdmans Publishing Company, 1960.